HOW TO RAISE AND TRAIN A BASENJI

By Jack Shafer and Bob Mankey

Distributed in the U.S.A. by T.F.H. Publications, Inc., 211 West Sylvania Avenue, P.O. Box 27, Neptune City, N.J. 07753; in England by T.F.H. (Gt. Britain) Ltd., 13 Nutley Lane, Reigate, Surrey; in Canada by Clarke, Irwin & Company, Clarwin House, 791 St. Clair Avenue West, Toronto 10, Ontario; in Southeast Asia by Y. W. Ong, 9 Lorong 36 Geylang, Singapore 14; in Australia and the south Pacific by Pet Imports Pty. Ltd., P.O. Box 149, Brookvale 2100, N.S.W., Australia.
Published by T.F.H. Publications, Inc. Ltd., The British Crown Colony of Hong Kong.

Frontispiece: The Basenji is one of the oldest existing dog breeds. He was the favorite pet of the Pharoahs and was the highly esteemed hunting companion of the Pygmies in Congo rain forests. Photo by Joan Ludwig.

ISBN 0-87666-239-4

©1966 by TFH PUBLICATIONS, INC.   P.O.Box 27, Neptune City, N.J. 07753

Contents

1. **HISTORY, DESCRIPTION, AND STANDARD** 5
   The Unique Basenji . . . Appearance and Temperament . . . The Basenji in England . . . The Basenji in America . . . Standard of the Basenji
2. **ENVIRONMENT AND MANAGEMENT** 21
   Special Early Training . . . Leads and Collars . . . Climatic Limitations and Housing . . . Feeding
3. **GROOMING** 26
   Ease of Care . . . Bathing . . . The Perfect Companion
4. **THE NEW PUPPY** 28
   Preparing for the Puppy's Arrival . . . Male or Female? . . . Where to Buy Your Puppy . . . Signs of Good Health . . . Age at Which Puppy Should Be Purchased . . . Papers . . . The Puppy's First Night With You . . . Your Puppy's Bed . . . Feeding Your Puppy . . . Transitional Diet . . . Breaking to Collar and Leash . . . Disciplining Your Puppy . . . Housebreaking . . . Outdoor Housebreaking
5. **TRAINING** 34
   When to Start Training . . . Your Part in Training . . . The Training Voice . . . Training Lessons . . . Your Training Equipment and Its Use . . . Heeling . . . "Heel" Means "Sit," Too . . . Training to Sit . . . The "Lie Down" . . . The "Stay" . . . The "Come" on Command . . . Teaching to Come to Heel . . . The "Stand" . . . Training Schools and Classes . . . Advanced Training and Obedience Trials
6. **BREEDING** 42
   The Question of Spaying . . . Sexual Physiology . . . Care of the Female in Estrus . . . Should You Breed Your Male? . . . Should You Breed Your Female? . . . When to Breed . . . How to Select a Stud . . . Preparation for Breeding . . . How Often Should You Breed Your Female? . . . The Importance and Application of Genetics
7. **CARE OF THE MOTHER AND FAMILY** 52
   Prenatal Care of the Female . . . Preparation of Whelping Quarters . . . Supplies to Have on Hand . . . Whelping . . . Raising the Puppies . . . How to Take Care of a Large Litter . . . Caesarean Section

8. HEALTH 56
   Watching Your Puppy's Health ... The Useful Thermometer ... First Aid ... Importance of Inoculations ... Distemper ... Hepatitis ... Leptospirosis ... Rabies ... Coughs, Colds, Bronchitis, Pneumonia ... Internal Parasites ... External Parasites ... Skin Ailments ... Eyes, Ears, Teeth, and Claws ... Care of the Aged Dog
9. SHOWING 61
   Types of Dog Shows ... How to Enter ... Advanced Preparation ... The Day of the Show
BIBLIOGRAPHY 64

1. History, Description, and Standard

THE UNIQUE BASENJI

In these modern times with man looking to the planets and new worlds to conquer . . . with modern science announcing fantastic new feats . . . the electronics age upon us with everything new, it seems strange that one of the breeds of purebred dogs that is advancing in popularity the fastest is a "new" breed of dog that dates back to the days of the Pharaohs and ancient Egypt.

Ch. Congo's Moja of Cambria, owned by Clyde D. and Aeola O'Harn. This sleek red and white male was best of breed at the Reno Kennel Club under judge Fred M. Hunt, handler Bob Mankey. Photo by Joan Ludwig.

So then, we find modern man of our century can cavort playfully with his "new" breed of dog just as the Egyptians of the IV Dynasty did in their courts. For engravings show that this "new" breed has a family tree that dates back to some early Egyptian engravings of 3600 B.C.

The breed is a medium-sized one that has found a new world of popularity with people who are situated in three rooms and a bath with neighbors on both sides who object to noisy dogs.

It is a breed of dog whose quietness can be guaranteed and whose shedding is of such short hairs that a few missed in the regular vacuuming wouldn't cause anyone to turn down an invitation to your home. It is a breed of dog that can be dried from a damp day's airing in just a short time and whose cleanliness is such that no objectionable odor ever exists!

This Twentieth Century miracle . . . this unique modern "dream world" dog is a breed of hound imported from Africa, called the Basenji.

The Basenji is what is termed a "natural breed" of great antiquity, in that he has not been altered to suit the modern whims and fancies of mankind.

The value of a good bitch is in the quality of her offspring. Ch. Cambria's Tabooo (far left) is shown winning a brood bitch class with five of her winning children: (l. to r.) Tabooo, Ch. Cambria's Nyakatii, Ch. Cambria's Ti-Jabu, Ch. Cambria's Batumba, Ch. Cambria's Ti-Kobra, and Cambria's Ti-Orpheus. The judge is Canadian breed authority, Sheila Anderson. Photo by Joan Ludwig.

Ch. Phemister's Kedar, owned by Cambria Kennels and bred by Mr. and Mrs. Alexander Phemister. Kedar was one of the first Basenjis to score top wins in interbreed competition. His record on the bench helped call attention to the breed when it was very new to shows and the quality of his offspring has helped the Basenji to new prestige among dog breeds throughout the country.

Ch. Cambria's Queen Xiote, owned by Phillis Shoop, with whom she is pictured, The Basenji has often been described as being deerlike both in appearance and in the grace of its movement. One look at this Basenji will show why the breed is so described.

The Basenji of today is basically the same regal picture he was when he was the favorite of the courts of the Pharaohs. In his native habitat the Basenji is used by the pygmies of the Ituri Forest as a running (finding and chasing), hunting dog and he is in great favor with the natives in that his scenting ability is so remarkable and for his cleanliness and (important in hunting) his lack of body odor.

The natives treat their Basenjis with such favor that they carry them about the neck, letting them "ride" to where the hunt is to be and if the weather becomes inclement, it is not unusual to find the natives out of their huts leaving the cover to their Basenjis.

APPEARANCE AND TEMPERAMENT

The Basenji is a short-coated, small, lightly built, short backed, regal appearing dog, with long legs, and fine bone structure. In profile the Basenji is a "square dog" in that the measurement from the top of his withers to the ground is approximately equal to, or only slightly less than, his overall body length. His short body and his habit of standing with his feet well

In 1956, Warner Brothers Pictures released a full-length movie entitled **Good-Bye My Lady** based on James Street's **Weep No More My Lady**. The film featured Walter Brennan and Brandon deWilde and served to make the Basenji many thousands of new friends.

under him permits rapid turning and dodging and has contributed to his survival in his native forests. The average height is 16 to 17 inches at the withers and the weight averages about 24 pounds.

There are three colors in the Basenji: red and white; black, tan and white or tri-color; and black and white. The basic body color of the Basenji is either red or black. Regardless of the basic color, all Basenjis should have white tail tips, white feet and white chests. The amount of white on the face, neck, shoulders, underparts and legs is optional.

Each of the color varieties has a wrinkled forehead. When alert, with upright ears pricked forward, there should be a fine, profuse wrinkle. Wrinkles are more pronounced in puppies, and because of the lack of shadowing, are not as noticeable in tri-colors or black and whites. The whole demeanor of the Basenji is one of poise and alertness.

The Basenji *is* and *should be* an intelligent animal, elegant looking and moving proudly with a gazelle-like grace.

He has been referred to as the "Barkless Dog," and this reference is correct, for the breed is naturally barkless! They are not, however, entirely mute for they can make many sounds common to all dogs. They do have a

Ch. Cambria's Kayfin, owned and bred by Cambria Kennels. Sire: Ch. Bettina's Oryx dam: Ch. My Love of the Congo. A homebred, this red and white is shown scoring a breed win under judge Vincent Perry, handler Bob Mankey. Photo by Joan Ludwig.

Ch. Cambria's Ti-Ngoma, owned by Cliff Pahlmann and bred by Cambria Kennels. Sire: Ch. Bettina's Oryx; dam: Ch. My Love of the Congo. This typey tri-color is shown scoring at the Basenji Club of America specialty under judge Alva Rosenberg, handler John Levy. The trophy is being presented by the celebrated jazz pianist and composer, Errol Garner. Photo by Bennett Associates.

friendly substitute for the bark, it is a sort of chortle or yodeling sound and to hear them emit this sound when playing is a joy.

As puppies they *can* whine or cry, but after the usual puppy sounds and correct training by the owner, people are amazed at how quiet they can be.

Even though he is a "barkless dog" it has been asked many times, "Is he then a watchdog?" I'd like to see any stranger or intruder come upon your home or yard with the Basenji there to guard it. He can make a noise, one which is seldom heard, but when he does you know that something is surely wrong. Picture an intruder face-to-face with a Basenji, his hair up on his back, his teeth showing and a deep rumbling growl emanating from his throat. This is sure to discourage anyone bent on trouble.

Children love Basenjis and Basenjis love children even more. They can play together for many hours, romping playfully and tirelessly together. When the evening hours come and the adults of the family want the more docile family pet, one to lay at the feet or on the couch next to them, the Basenji loves the relaxation of their company and plays in his own different way for the elders of the household.

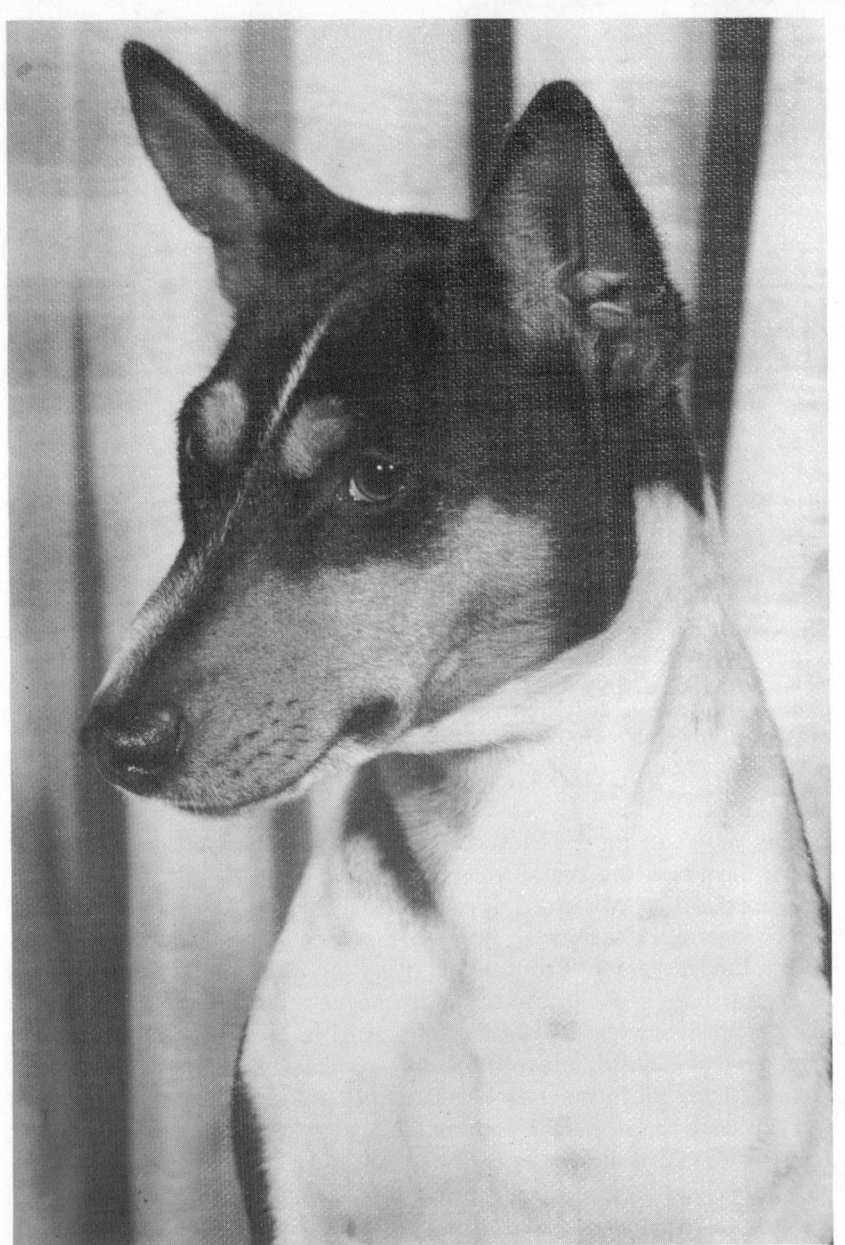

Ch. Ti-Kimuria of Cambria, owned by Nazrat Kennels. Sire: Ch. Cambria's Ti-Mungai; dam: Ch. Cambria's Ti-Zenda. The Basenji is distinctive in many ways aside from his lack of a bark. His combination of unique characteristics has made him a much-sought-after pet and companion.

The breed rarely ever requires bathing and Basenjis actually clean themselves as does a cat! Another nice feature Basenji owners discover is that they rarely have more than a minimum of a flea or bug problem.

It is a pleasure to note the distinctive Basenji gait . . . for when they walk slowly they are like a trotting horse and their faster gait is like that of a gazelle.

Basenjis, when very sad, have been known to cry real tears. This occurs many times to the female, during the breeding or whelping process.

THE BASENJI IN ENGLAND

In the *Illustrated Kennel News* of England of 1908 there was a picture of native dogs from the Congo and this was in reference to dogs exhibited at the Crufts Show of 1895. The dogs which appeared as "Basenji-like" were entered and exhibited as *African Bush Dogs* (also known as Congo Terriers). These dogs were purchased at the show by a W. R. Temple who was then an associate of H. C. Brooke who was considered to be one of the foremost

Ch. Cambria's Ti-Kobra, owned and bred by Cambria Kennels. Sire: Ch. Cambria's Ti-Mungai; dam: Ch. Cambria's Tabooo. This tri-color homebred is shown scoring a best of breed win under judge Chris Shuttleworth, handler Jack Shafer. Photo by Joan Ludwig.

experts on foreign dogs. These dogs died a short time after the show, having contracted distemper. Early informants on research and information on the breed stated also that there was a pair of the same breed exhibited at approximately the same time at the *Jardin d'Acclimatation* in Paris, France.

Basenjis fell to the wayside from this time until the year 1923 when Lady Helen Nutting became enamored with the Zande Dogs, from a region of the Nile, that were favored dogs of the natives. She later transported six of these dogs to England but the distemper shots given them caused them to fall ill after arriving in England and they later died.

Again following the demise of the six, the Basenji became all but a forgotten breed until they were again transported to England from the Belgian Congo and shown at several shows in England that year. The exhibitor had been chided by some fellow exhibitors that she had crossed the Corgi and the Bull Terrier to produce this "new" breed.

Like puppies of all breeds, Basenji puppies have a great degree of charm about them. The breed's characteristic quizzical expression gives Basenji puppies something extra.

Most Basenjis are either red and white or tri-color. All should have wrinkled foreheads, but this will be more easily seen on reds and not as evident on tris. Photo by Joan Ludwig.

Finally, after much difficulty, the experts of the London Zoo and the experts of the Kennel Club agreed to the purebred aspects of the dogs and thus they were registered under the breed name "Basenji." In the Inter-Territorial Swahili Dictionaries the closest translation is "Wilde Thing" or "Bushe Thing."

One of the people most responsible for the success and the basic lines of the Basenji was in England; her name was Veronica Tudor-Williams and to this day Mrs. Tudor-Williams is considered one of the great experts on the Basenji. In 1941 she acquired an exceptional red and white female named

Amatangazig. Mrs. Tudor-Williams has stated that without the influence of Amatangazig of the Congo on the breed, the breed could have faded out or taken many years longer to be developed. This famous bitch passed away at the age of 14 on New Year's Day of 1952.

The actual listing of the dogs that are considered the "foundation stock" of the breed coming from Africa were Bongo of Blean, Bokoto of Blean, Bashele of Blean, Bereke of Blean, Bungwa of Blean and Bakuma of Blean. They were brought to England by another of the famous founders of the breed, Mrs. Oliver Burn, between 1936 and 1937. All of these dogs, with the exception of Bakuma, remained in England to become the foundation stock of the "Blean Kennels" and the "— of the Congo" Kennels of Veronica Tudor-Williams. Bakuma later was acquired by two of the founders of the breed in the United States, Mr. and Mrs. Alexander Phemister of Kingston, Massachusetts.

THE BASENJI IN AMERICA

In April of 1941, a tramp steamer from the Western coast of Africa (possibly Leopoldville) arrived in Boston. In the hold of that ship Alexander Phemister found a Basenji bitch that had been there for almost three weeks. Phemister, who acquired the bitch, said that her condition was such that she weighed only nine pounds on arrival. The next dogs out of Africa were Kindu and Kasenyi who arrived in the summer of 1941 along with a shipload of gorillas and other animals for a Henry Trefflich of New York. In 1952, Veronica Tudor-Williams imported Wau of the Congo from the Southern Sudan and then a few years later she journeyed to Africa and brought back with her Fula of the Congo. Thus, with the elimination of the dog known as "Simolo" from the early pedigrees, these were the basic dogs that are and should be considered the foundation stock of the American Basenji.

In 1937 a Mrs. Rogers brought Bakuma of Blean to New York. In the early summer of 1941 the Alexander Phemisters acquired Bakuma and registered him with the American Kennel Club as Phemister's Bois. The next Basenjis who arrived in the United States for breeding purposes were all dogs from the "— of the Congo" strain, named Kwillo, Kikuyu, Koodoo and Kitreve. They all went to a Dr. Richmond and thus the first litter of Basenjis born in America was by Koodoo x Kikuyu. The first litter sired by a United States' dog was by Phemister's Bois x Phemister's Naida (a daughter of Phemister's Congo). It was in June of 1941 that another of the early founders of the breed in this country acquired his first Basenji. George Gilkey purchased a bitch from Dr. Richmond named Tanya of Windrush. The Basenji Club of America accepted the Standard of the breed as drawn up by the Basenji Club of England. The American Kennel Club then, in 1943, accepted this Standard as official and thus accepted the Basenji as acceptable for registration in the AKC Stud Book. Basenjis were shown at the Westminster Kennel Club show

Ch. Cambria's Ti-Mungai, owned and bred by Cambria Kennels. Sire: Ch. Bettina's Oryx; dam: Ch. My Love of the Congo. This handsome dog is the top winning tri in the breed and is also the sire of 26 champions. He is a record holder both as a winner and as a producer. Photo by Joan Ludwig.

in 1945 with an entry of five. They were shown in the Miscellaneous Class. The first time a Basenji was shown in the United States in the Hound Group was on June 3, 1945, at the Orange Empire show in California.

The foundation stock of the authors' Cambria Kennels in Santa Ana, California, was first acquired from the Phemisters with the purchase of Ch. Katema of Carmel and Ch. Phemisters Kedar. Kedar became one of the all time top-winning Basenjis in the early history of the breed and lived in retirement at Cambria until his death in June 1966. Among others in the foundation stock of Cambria were the Irish import, Ch. Victory of Syngefield; Ch. My Love of the Congo, who was the dam of 15 American Champions and the tricolor Ch. Bettina's Oryx. The breeding combination of Oryx and My Love produced the all time winning tri-color Ch. Cambria's Ti-Mungai who, as of this writing, has produced the record amount of champions—26!

In April 1942, a story by James Street appeared in the Saturday Evening Post titled "Weep No More My Lady," and this later became a novel "Goodbye My Lady" which was in turn produced as a feature movie by Warner Brothers Pictures and helped immeasurably in the new popularity of the breed.

STANDARD OF THE BASENJI

Characteristics: The Basenji should not bark, but is not mute. The wrinkled forehead and the swift, tireless running gait (resembling a race horse trotting full out) are typical of the breed.

General Appearance: The Basenji is a small, lightly built, short backed dog, giving the impression of being high on the leg compared to its length. The wrinkled head must be proudly carried, and the whole demeanor should be one of poise and alertness.

Head and Skull: The skull is flat, well chiseled and of medium width, tapering toward the eyes. The foreface should taper from eye to muzzle and should be shorter than the skull. Muzzle, neither coarse, nor snipy but with rounded cushions. Wrinkles should appear upon the forehead, and be fine and profuse. Side wrinkles are desirable, but should never be exaggerated into dewlap.

Nose: Black greatly desired. A pinkish tinge should not penalize an otherwise first class specimen, but it should be discouraged in breeding.

Eyes: Dark hazel, almond shaped, obliquely set and far seeing.

Ears: Small, pointed and erect, of fine texture, set well forward on top of head.

Mouth: Teeth must be level with scissors bite.

Neck: Of good length, well crested and slightly full at base of throat. It should be well set into flat, laid back shoulders.

Forequarters: The chest should be deep and of medium width. The legs

Ch. Cambria's Tacuba, owned and bred by Cambria Kennels. Tacuba has the distinction of being the 50th homebred champion for Cambria Kennels. Photo by Joan Ludwig.

straight with clean fine bone, long forearm and well defined sinews. Pasterns should be of good length, straight and flexible.

Body: The body should be short and the back level. The ribs well sprung, with plenty of heart room, deep brisket, short coupled, and ending in a definite waist.

Hindquarters: Should be strong and muscular, with hocks well let down, turned neither in nor out, with long second thighs.

Feet: Small, narrow and compact, with well arched toes.

Tail: Should be set on top and curled tightly over to either side.

Coat: Short and silky. Skin very pliant.

Color: Chestnut red (the deeper the better) or pure black, or black and tan, all with white feet, chest and tail tip. White legs, white blaze and white collar optional.

Weight: Bitches 22 pounds approximately. Dogs 24 pounds.

Size: Bitches 16 inches and dogs 17 inches from the ground to the top of the shoulder. Bitches 16 inches and dogs 17 inches from the front of the chest to the farthest point of the hindquarters.

Faults: Coarse skull or muzzle. Domed or peaked skull. Dewlap. Round eyes. Low set ears. Overshot or undershot mouths. Wide chest. Wide behind. Heavy bone. Creams, shaded or off colors, other than those defined above, should be heavily penalized.

The Basenji's appearance suggests great vitality. This is not misleading for the Basenji loves to climb and jump, and run as proven by this action photo of Ch. Phemister's Kedar sailing over some shrubbery.

2. Environment and Management

The Basenji is one of the few breeds of purebred dogs that can fit so well into a variety of different type homes. For the apartment dweller the Basenji can accept the daily walks on leash with the master as all of the exercise he needs or seems to want. He can play tirelessly in the home only to rest when the master of the house says to rest. Those who have large yards will find the fun, playing attitude of the Basenji a real joy, for the breed's outlook while playing is so unique that one must almost have to witness the breed in action to believe it.

Ch. Cambria's Tabooo, owned by Cambria Kennels. Sire: Ch. Cambria's Hamen; dam: Ch. My Love of the Congo. This red and white is one of the top-producing bitches of the breed as well as being a winner in her own right. Photo by Joan Ludwig.

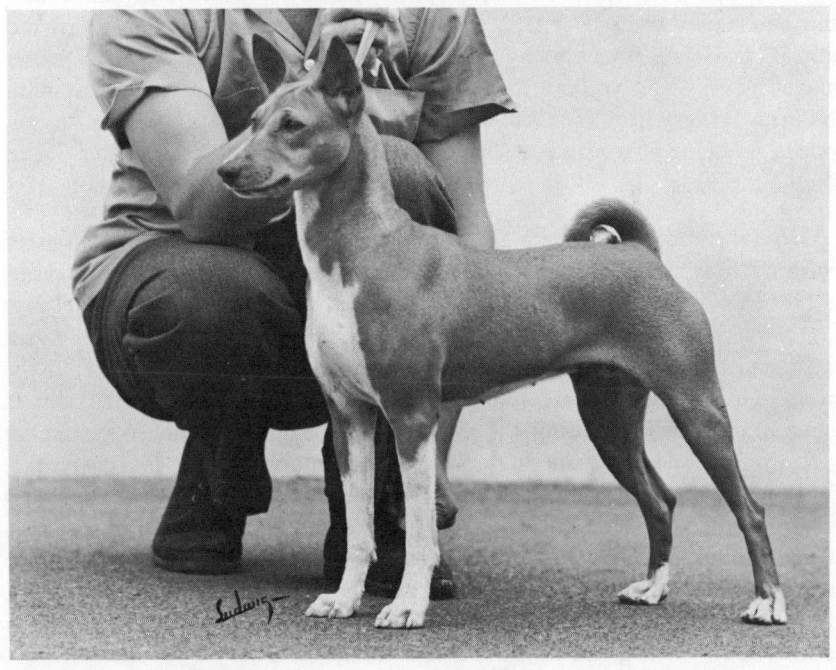

SPECIAL EARLY TRAINING

Having bred and raised many Basenjis we have become firm in the fact that the breed *must* be trained young. Any obedience instructor will argue that you do not start training the puppy until the puppy is at least six months of age. This is far from true with the Basenji. We have learned long ago that four months is the perfect time. Be firm with your voice in training, *do not* at any time let the puppy train you . . . you train the puppy. Once the Basenji puppy has learned, he retains it. Remember that he can also learn (young) that he can run . . . so if you have a problem puppy it is the fault of the owners, *not* the pup! Oddly enough, and sometimes hard to convince people of, it is easier to own two Basenji puppies, male and female, than any breed we have ever known. They can play together perfectly and can, oddly enough, train each other to what you want. It is great fun to watch two Basenjis busy at the task of bathing each other. Basenjis can climb if they want to, so do not think that a four or five foot chain link fence is going to keep your Basenji at home. It's fun to watch the young puppy learning how to put his paws in the rings of the fence, but stop him from that fun early, or you'll be sorry.

LEADS AND COLLARS

Put a soft leather collar on your puppy at an early age and keep one on him until he is used to it. If he tries to scratch it off, don't feel sorry for him and take it off. He's getting his way then. Start lead training when he is still young and if he cries and you fall for it, you'll have a problem leash training him. Be firm. Be very firm. You *will* not and cannot break the spirit of the Basenji puppy by being firm with him. He'll like you for it and will be a better dog in the long run.

Do not put a harness on a Basenji. A good leather collar and a lead fitted with a strong snap is advisable. The Basenji is a small dog yes, but he packs a lot of power in that small package. When showing the Basenji we always use a chain collar and a show lead looped into the chain. It is enjoyable to see a Basenji moving full out. It is not enjoyable to see him dragged about the ring, choking and gagging as he goes. Obedience training can help out in show training. When using the chain collar the first few times, remember that the Basenji is fast, not only in movement but on backing up on you too. Without proper care and instruction you can be left holding a lead and a chain while your Basenji is playfully cavorting around his training area. Once your Basenji has learned to move on his chain collar, let the lead drop and the chain fall loose, thus letting your dog have his own free movement. It is suggested that you move just a little ahead of the dog, keeping your attention on the dog and in this way, his attention is on y

Ch. Cambria's Nyakatii, owned by Cambria Kennels. A home-bred, he was chosen best of breed at the Westminster Kennel Club by judge Fred M. Hunt and was handled by Bob Mankey. Nyakatii subsequently placed fourth in the hound group. Photo by William Gilbert.

Ch. Cambria's Bwasisi, owned and bred by Cambria Kennels. Sire: Ch. Bwana of the Congo; dam: Ch. Cambria's Aomon Isis. This bitch was best of breed at Chicago International under judge Charles F. Kellogg and was handled by Bob Mankey. Photo by Evelyn Shafer.

Cambria's Askari, owned by Donald Truitt. The Basenji's great ease of care is another factor that has helped to greatly popularize the breed. He is a good doer and most adaptable to any home and atmosphere.

CLIMATIC LIMITATIONS AND HOUSING

Basenjis have made their homes all over the world, but they like warmth. This is particularly true with the puppies. Basenjis, as youngsters, must be kept warm and dry. As adults they can acclimate themselves to most any temperature, but it is not surprising to find your Basenji sleeping practically in a fireplace or on top of a heater register. As to warm spots of sunshine, they can lie for hours enjoying the warmth of the sun whereas other breeds would have been panting looking for the nearest shade. Many owners of Basenjis have found that they do better with the type of crate used for benching dogs at dog shows, rather than the conventional dog beds. These metal crates, which can be collapsed when not in use, can be purchased from most larger pet shops or can be ordered should the shop not have them in stock.

As to the coat on the Basenji, we have noticed as far as different areas, that the Basenjis in the colder areas tend to have a heavier or thicker undercoat. Without proper care (which we will go into in the next chapter) in warmer areas, the coat of the Basenji can be dried and look dead without the right additives and equipment. We do not feel that there is any area where a Basenji cannot live comfortably and happily, with the owners giving maximum attention to proper feeding of vitamins and good housing.

FEEDING

Basenjis are eager eaters and do well with a good type dry food mixed with uncooked beef. It has been found that horse meat is often too rich for the Basenji. Most pet shops now feature good varieties of beef, either fresh frozen or canned. The choice of a good one of these beef products to be mixed with the dry food is the basis of the perfect diet for the Basenji.

We have always considered the vitamins and coat additives for pets as the best form of insurance for a healthy, happy and eye-appealing dog. The coat of the Basenji when he has been raised and fed properly with the right additives is one that glistens and feels comfortable to the touch. The dry, shedding coat is a good sign that the right additives are missing in the daily diet. Don't try to save a cent or two when buying the vitamins and oils for your Basenji. Buy the best (they don't cost that much more) and the results will be more than worthwhile. Do not fall to the appealing eyes of your Basenji when you are at your dining table. Make him learn young that his dinner is his dinner and that yours is yours! In other words, don't pamper him with several bits of steak, then he picks at his food, thus failing to get those vitamins you mixed in with the food. As mentioned earlier, you be the boss!

3. Grooming

EASE OF CARE

How fortunate you are with a Basenji when it comes to the grooming. With the short hair and the way they like to keep themselves clean, *all the time*, it is no problem to maintain and keep him looking always in the peak of condition. Your grooming takes but a short time to do. If you can arrange to allot yourself a few minutes each day to rub him down with a small amount of dog grooming oil, then work over his coat from the ears to the rear with a rubber curry brush, your Basenji will be show ring ready every day and will have no problems with coat or skin disorders.

A day prior to showing your Basenji, oil his coat down heavily and, should his white parts be dull, chalk them. Use a soft brush (as the type used for brushing a cat) to remove all of the chalk. Wipe the oil off with a damp wash towel. When he is dry, a light coat of oil spray makes him gleam for the ring.

Be sure you have trimmed his whiskers off using the eye and nose pet scissors your pet dealer has for this purpose.

The claws should be shortened several days before the show and then filed regularly. A Basenji with long claws looks bad and the condition tends to make his foot look poorly if the claws are so long as to touch the ground.

A few "wild" hairs may have to be trimmed around the tail, but great caution should be used in doing this if you are not familiar with the system. Many breeders or handlers could show the novice the correct way to do this.

The Basenji's beautifully erect ears can also be dust and dirt catchers. Therefore, don't forget to clean the ears. Ear drops for pets can be dropped in the ear and a Q-tip used to clean inside, but a word of caution here too... only use the type of Q-tip that would be used for babies... that is the flexible type, not the hard, stick type and never go deeper than you can see.

BATHING

It is rare that you will have to bathe your Basenji, but should the need arise, *never* use your own favorite human shampoo for the purpose. Use a good quality pet shampoo, preferably one that is non-toxic. This same care should be given to the use of flea sprays on and around Basenjis. Remember, your Basenji cleans himself as a cat does. In other words, the spray that is used must be of the non-toxic type or a cat type spray. By following this rule, much trouble can be avoided in the health of your Basenji.

The sleek appearance of a Basenji is easy to bring about with good grooming. This grooming though, should start with the young puppy. In this way the dog will be accustomed to the attention and always look forward to being groomed. Photo by Louise Van der Meid.

As far as grooming a Basenji is concerned, it is no problem. Just use the proper equipment for what has to be done, give the dog the proper vitamins and the best in coat additives and the few minutes a day from you . . . the result is just what you would want to see.

THE PERFECT COMPANION

Your Basenji, trained correctly, fed correctly and reared correctly can be a marvelous companion for the family. He is unlike any other breed of dog. He is a joy to own and behold. In retrospect, we again urge every person who acquires a Basenji puppy to follow the suggestions regarding proper obedience training, proper food and proper vitamins along with the correct grooming aids. Your pet dealers can assist you in these departments. Your Basenji will be a fun and pleasure for many years to come.

4. The New Puppy

PREPARING FOR THE PUPPY'S ARRIVAL

Because at least three out of four prospective purchasers of dogs want to buy a young rather than an adult or almost adult dog, the problem of preparing for the arrival of a permanent canine house guest almost always means preparing for the arrival of a puppy. This is not to say that there is anything wrong with purchasing an adult dog; on the contrary, such a purchase has definite advantages in that it often allows freedom from housebreaking chores and rigorous feeding schedules, and these are of definite benefit to prospective purchasers who have little time to spare. Since the great majority of dog buyers, however, prefer to watch their pet grow from sprawlingly playful puppyhood to dignified maturity, buying a dog, practically speaking, means buying a puppy.

Before you get a puppy be sure that you are willing to take the responsibility of training him and caring for his physical needs. His early training is most important, as an adult dog that is a well-behaved member of the family is the end product of your early training. Remember that your new puppy knows only a life of romping with his littermates and the security of being with his mother, and that coming into your home is a new and sometimes frightening experience for him. He will adjust quickly if you are patient with him and show him what you expect of him. If there are small children in the family be sure that they do not abuse him or play roughly with him. A puppy plays hard, but he also requires frequent periods of rest. Before he comes, decide where he is to sleep and where he is to eat. If your puppy does not have a collar, find out the size he requires and buy an inexpensive one, as he will soon outgrow it. Have the proper grooming equipment on hand. Consult the person from whom you bought the puppy as to the proper food for your puppy, and learn the feeding time and amount that he eats a day. Buy him some toys—usually the breeder will give you some particular toy or toys which he has cherished as a puppy to add to his new ones and to make him less homesick. Get everything you need from your petshop *before* you bring the puppy home.

MALE OR FEMALE?

Before buying your puppy you should have made a decision as to whether you want a male or a female. Unless you want to breed your pet and raise a litter of puppies, your preference as to the sex of your puppy is strictly a personal choice. Both sexes are pretty much the same in disposition and character, and both make equally good pets.

WHERE TO BUY YOUR PUPPY

Although petshop owners are necessarily restricted from carrying all breeds in stock, they know the best dog breeders and are sometimes able to supply quality puppies on demand. In cases in which a petshop owner is unable to obtain a dog for you, he can still refer you to a good source, such as a reputable kennel. If your local petshop proprietor is unable to either obtain a dog for you or refer you to someone from whom you can purchase one, don't give up: there are other avenues to explore. The American Kennel Club will furnish you addresses. Additional sources of information are the various magazines devoted to the dog fancy.

SIGNS OF GOOD HEALTH

Picking out a healthy, attractive little fellow to join the family circle is a different matter from picking a show dog; it is also a great deal less complicated. Often the puppy will pick you. If he does, and it is mutual admiration at first sight, he is the best puppy for you. At a reliable kennel or petshop the owner will be glad to answer your questions and to point out the difference between pet and show-quality puppies. Trust your eyes and hands to tell if the puppies are sound in body and temperament. Ears and eyes should not have suspicious discharges. Legs should have strong bones; bodies should have solid muscles. Coats should be clean. Lift the hair to see if the skin is free of scales and parasites.

Temperament can vary from puppy to puppy in the same litter. There is always one puppy which will impress you by his energy and personality. He loves to show off and will fling himself all over you and his littermates, and everyone who comes to see the puppies falls in love with him. However, do not overlook the more reserved puppy. Most dogs are wary of strangers, so reserve may indicate caution, not a timid puppy. He may calmly accept your presence when he senses that all is well. Such a puppy should be a steady reliable dog when mature. In any event, never force yourself on a puppy — let him come to you. Reliable breeders and petshops will urge you to take your puppy to the veterinarian of your choice to have the puppy's health checked, and will allow you at least two days in which to have it done. It should be clearly understood whether rejection by a veterinarian for health reasons means that you have the choice of another puppy from that litter or that you get your money back.

AGE AT WHICH PUPPY SHOULD BE PURCHASED

A puppy should be at least six weeks of age before you take him home. Many breeders will not let puppies go before they are two months old. In general, the puppy you buy for show and breeding should be five or six months old. If you want a show dog, remember that not even an expert can predict with 100% accuracy what a small puppy will be when he grows up.

PAPERS

When you buy a purebred dog you should receive his American Kennel Club registration certificate (or an application form to fill out), a pedigree, and a health certificate made out by the breeder's veterinarian. The registration certificate is the official A.K.C. paper. If the puppy was named and registered by his breeder you will want to complete the transfer and send it, with the fee, to the American Kennel Club. They will transfer the dog to your ownership in their records and send a new certificate to you. If you receive, instead, an application for registration, you should fill it out, choosing a name for your dog, and mail it, with the fee, to the A.K.C.

The pedigree is a chart showing your puppy's ancestry and is not a part of his official papers. The health certificate will tell what shots have been given and when the next ones are due. Your veterinarian will be appreciative of this information, and will continue with the same series of shots if they have not been completed. The health certificate will also give the dates on which the puppy has been wormed. Ask your veterinarian whether rabies shots are required in your locality. Most breeders will give you food for a few days along with instructions for feeding so that your puppy will have the same diet he is accustomed to until you can buy a supply at your petshop.

THE PUPPY'S FIRST NIGHT WITH YOU

The puppy's first night at home is likely to be disturbing to the family. Keep in mind that suddenly being away from his mother, brothers, and sisters is a new experience for him; he may be confused and frightened. If you have a special room in which you have his bed, be sure that there is nothing there with which he can harm himself. Be sure that all lamp cords are out of his reach and that there is nothing that he can tip or pull over. Check furniture that he might get stuck under or behind and objects that he might chew. If you want him to sleep in your room he probably will be quiet all night, reassured by your presence. If left in a room by himself he will cry and howl, and you will have to steel yourself to be impervious to his whining. After a few nights alone he will adjust. The first night that he is alone it is wise to put a loud-ticking alarm clock, as well as his toys, in the room with him. The alarm clock will make a comforting noise, and he will not feel that he is alone.

YOUR PUPPY'S BED

Every dog likes to have a place that is his alone. He holds nothing more sacred than his own bed whether it be a rug, dog crate, or dog bed. If you get your puppy a bed be sure to get one which discourages chewing. Also be sure that the bed is large enough to be comfortable for him when he is fully grown. Locate it away from drafts and radiators. A word might be said here in defense of the crate, which many pet owners think is cruel and confining. Given a choice, a young dog instinctively selects a secure place

Special dog feeding and watering utensils are so designed as to safeguard your pet from dangerous porcelain chips. These utensils are easy to keep clean, too.

in which to lounge, rest, or sleep. The walls and ceiling of a crate, even a wire one, answer that need. Once he regards his crate as a safe and reassuring place to stay, you will be able to leave him alone in the house.

FEEDING YOUR PUPPY

As a general rule, a puppy from weaning time (six weeks) to three months of age should have *four meals a day;* from three months to six months, *three meals;* from six months to one year, *two meals.* After a year, a dog does well on *one meal daily.* There are as many feeding schedules as there are breeders, and puppies do fine on all of them, so it is best for the new owner to follow the one given him by the breeder of his puppy. Remember that all dogs are individuals. The amount that will keep your dog in good health is right for him, not the "rule-book" amount. A feeding schedule to give you some idea of what the average puppy will eat is as follows:

Morning meal: Puppy meal with milk.
Afternoon meal: Meat mixed with puppy meal, plus a vitamin-mineral supplement.
Evening meal: Same as afternoon meal, but without a vitamin-mineral supplement.

Do not change the amounts in your puppy's diet too rapidly. If he gets diarrhea it may be that he is eating too much, so cut back on his food and when he is normal again increase his food more slowly.

There is a canned food made especially for puppies which you can buy only by a veterinarian's prescription. Some breeders use this very successfully from weaning to three months.

TRANSITIONAL DIET

Changing over to an adult program of feeding is not difficult. Very often the puppy will change himself; that is, he will refuse to eat some of his meals. He adjusts to his one meal (or two meals) a day without any trouble at all.

BREAKING TO COLLAR AND LEASH

Puppies are usually broken to a collar before you bring them home, but even if yours has never worn one it is a simple matter to get him used to it. Put a loose collar on him for a few hours at a time. At first he may scratch at it and try to get it off, but gradually he will take it as a matter of course. To break him to a lead, attach his leash to his collar and let him drag it around. When he becomes used to it pick it up and gently pull him in the direction you want him to go. He will think it is a game, and with a bit of patience on your part he will allow himself to be led.

DISCIPLINING YOUR PUPPY

The way to have a well-mannered adult dog is to give him firm basic training while he is a puppy. When you say *"No"* you must mean *"No."* Your dog will respect you only if you are firm. A six- to eight-weeks-old puppy is old enough to understand what *"No"* means. The first time you see your puppy doing something he shouldn't be doing, chewing something he shouldn't chew, or wandering in a forbidden area, it's time to teach him. Shout, *"No."* Puppies do not like loud noises, and your misbehaving pet will readily connect the word with something unpleasant. Usually a firm *"No"* in a disapproving tone of voice is enough to correct your dog, but occasionally you get a puppy that requires a firmer hand, especially as he grows older. In this case hold your puppy firmly and slap him gently across the hindquarters. If this seems cruel, you should realize that no dog resents being disciplined if he is caught in the act of doing something wrong, and your puppy will be intelligent enough to know what the slap was for.

After you have slapped him and you can see that he has learned his lesson, call him to you and talk to him in a pleasant tone of voice — praise him for coming to you. This sounds contradictory, but it works with a puppy. He immediately forgives you, practically tells you that it was his fault and that he deserved his punishment, and promises that it will not happen again. This form of discipline works best and may be used for all misbehaviors.

Never punish your puppy by chasing him around, making occasional swipes with a rolled-up newspaper; punish him only when you have a firm hold on him. Above all, never punish your dog after having called him to you. He must learn to associate coming to you with something pleasant.

HOUSEBREAKING

While housebreaking your puppy do not let him have the run of the house. If you do you will find that he will pick out his own bathroom, which may be in your bedroom or in the middle of the living room rug. Keep him confined to a small area where you can watch him, and you will be able to train him much more easily and speedily. A puppy does not want to dirty his bed, but he does need to be taught where he should go. Spread papers over his living quarters, then watch him carefully. When you notice him starting to whimper, sniff the floor, or run agitatedly in little circles, rush him to the place that you want to serve as his relief area and gently hold him there until he relieves himself. Then praise him lavishly. When you remove the soiled papers, leave a small damp piece so that the puppy's sense of smell will lead him back there next time. If he makes a mistake, wash the area at once with warm water, followed by a rinse with water and vinegar or sudsy ammonia. This will kill the odor and prevent discoloration. It shouldn't take more than a few days for him to get the idea of using newspapers. When he becomes fairly consistent, reduce the area of paper to a few sheets in a corner. As soon as you think he has the idea fixed in his mind, you can let him roam around the house a bit, but keep an eye on him. It might be best to keep him on leash the first few days so that you can rush him back to his paper at any signs of an approaching accident.

The normal healthy puppy will want to relieve himself when he wakes up in the morning, after each feeding, and after strenuous exercise. During early puppyhood any excitement, such as the return home of a member of the family or the approach of a visitor, may result in floor-wetting, but that phase should pass in a few weeks. Keep in mind that you can't expect too much from your puppy until he is about five months old. Before that, his muscles and digestive system just aren't under his control.

OUTDOOR HOUSEBREAKING

You can begin outdoor training on leash even while you are paper-training your puppy. First thing in the morning take him outdoors (to the curb, if you are in the city) and walk him back and forth in a small area until he relieves himself. He will probably make a puddle and then walk around, uncertain of what is expected of him. You can try standing him over a newspaper, which may give him the idea. Some dog trainers use glycerine suppositories at this point for fast action. Praise your dog every time taking him outside brings results, and he will get the idea. You'll find, when you begin the outdoor training, that the male puppy usually requires a longer walk than the female. Both male and female puppies will squat. It isn't until he is older that the male dog will begin to lift his leg. If you hate to give up your sleep, you can train your puppy to go outdoors during the day and use the paper at night.

5. Training

WHEN TO START TRAINING

You should never begin SERIOUS obedience training before your dog is seven or eight months old. (Some animal psychologists state that puppies can begin training when seven weeks old, if certain techniques are followed. These techniques, however, are still experimental and should be left to the professional trainer to prove their worth.) While your dog is still in his early puppyhood, concentrate on winning his confidence so he will love and admire you. This will make his training easier, since he will do anything to please you. Basic training can be started at the age of three or four months. He should be taught to walk nicely on a leash, sit and lie down on command, and come when he is called.

YOUR PART IN TRAINING

You must patiently demonstrate to your dog what each word of command means. Guide him with your hands and the training leash, reassuring him with your voice, through whatever routine you are teaching him. Repeat the word associated with the act. Demonstrate again and again to give the dog a chance to make the connection in his mind.

Once he begins to get the idea, use the word of command without any physical guidance. Drill him. When he makes mistakes, correct him, kindly at first, more severely as his training progresses. Try not to lose your patience or become irritated, and never slap him with your hand or the leash during the training session. Withholding praise or rebuking him will make him feel bad enough.

When he does what you want, praise him lavishly with words and with pats. Don't continually reward with dog candy or treats in training. The dog that gets into the habit of performing for a treat will seldom be fully dependable when he can't smell or see one in the offing. When he carries out a command, even though his performance is slow or sloppy, praise him and he will perform more readily the next time.

THE TRAINING VOICE

When you start training your dog, use your training voice, giving commands in a firm, clear tone. Once you give a command, persist until it is obeyed, even if you have to pull the dog to obey you. He must learn that training is different from playing, that a command once given must be obeyed no matter what distractions are present. Remember that the tone and pitch of your voice, not loudness, are the qualities that will influence your dog most.

Be consistent in the use of words during training. Confine your commands to as few words as possible and never change them. It is best for only one person to carry on the dog's training, because different people will use different words and tactics that will confuse your dog. The dog who hears *"come," "get over here," "hurry up," "here, Rex,"* and other commands when he is wanted will become totally confused.

TRAINING LESSONS

Training is hard on the dog — and on the trainer. A young dog just cannot take more than ten minutes of training at a stretch, so limit the length of your first lessons. Then you can gradually increase the length of time to about thirty minutes. You'll find that you too will tend to become impatient when you stretch out a training lesson. If you find yourself losing your temper, stop and resume the lesson at another time. Before and after each lesson have a play period, but don't play during a training session. Even the youngest dog soon learns that schooling is a serious matter; fun comes afterward.

Don't spend too much time on one phase of the training, or the dog will become bored. Always try to end a lesson on a pleasant note. Actually, in nine cases out of ten, if your dog isn't doing what you want it's because you're not getting the idea over to him properly.

YOUR TRAINING EQUIPMENT AND ITS USE

The leash is more properly called the lead, so we'll use that term here. The best leads for training are the six-foot webbed-cloth leads, usually olive-drab in color, and the six-foot leather lead. Fancier leads are available and may be used if desired.

You'll need a metal-link collar, called a choke chain, consisting of a metal chain with rings on each end. Even though the name may sound frightening, it won't hurt your dog, and it is an absolute MUST in training. There is a right and a wrong way to put the training collar on. It should go around the dog's neck so that you can attach the lead to the ring at the end of the chain which passes OVER, not under his neck. It is most important that the collar is put on properly so it will tighten when the lead is pulled and ease when you relax your grip.

The correct way to hold the lead is also very important, as the collar should have some slack in it, at all times, except when correcting. Holding the loop in your right hand, extend your arm out to the side, even with your shoulder. With your left hand, grasp the lead as close as possible to the collar, without making it tight. The remaining portion of the lead can be made into a loop which is held in the right hand. Keep this arm close to your body. Most corrections will be made with the left hand by giving the lead a jerk in the direction you want the dog to go. The dog that pulls and forges ahead can be corrected by a steady pull on the lead.

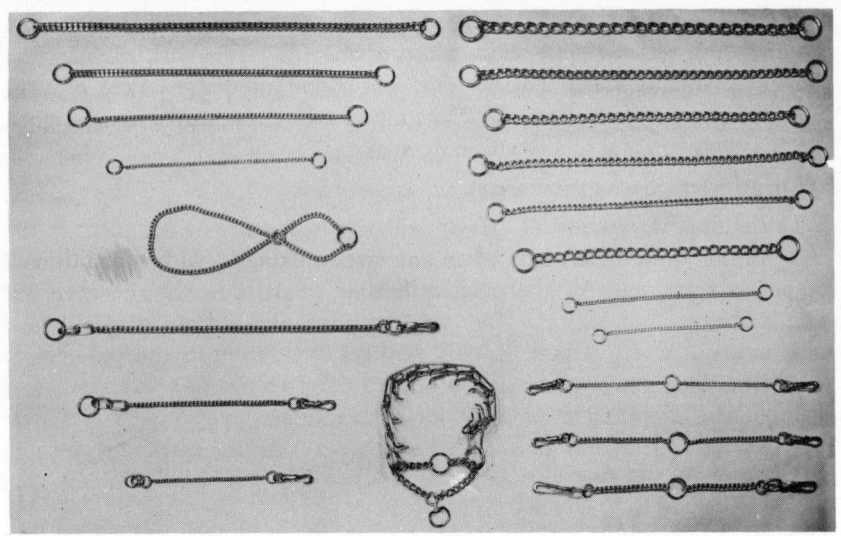

Special training collars for your dog can be purchased at your petshop.

HEELING

"Heeling" in dog language means having your dog walk alongside you on your left side, close to your leg, on lead or off. With patience and effort you can train your dog to walk with you even on a crowded street or in the presence of other dogs.

Now that you have learned the correct way to put on your dog's collar and how to hold the lead, you are ready to start with his first lesson in heeling. Put the dog at your left side, sitting. Using the dog's name and the command *"Heel,"* start forward on your LEFT foot, giving a tug on the lead to get the dog started. Always use the dog's name first, followed by the command, such as *"Rex, heel."* Saying his name will help get his attention and will let him know that you are about to give a command.

Walk briskly, with even steps, going around in a large circle, square, or straight line. While walking, make sure that your dog stays on the left side and close to your leg. If he lags behind, give several tugs on the lead to get him up to you, then praise him for doing well. If he forges ahead or swings wide, stop and jerk the lead sharply and bring him back to the proper position. Always repeat the command when correcting, and praise him when he does well. If your dog continues to pull or lag behind, either your corrections are not severe enough or your timing between correction and praise is off. Do this exercise for only five minutes at first, gradually lengthening it to fifteen, or even half an hour.

To keep your dog's attention, talk to him as you keep him in place. You can also do a series of fast about-turns, giving the lead a jerk as you turn. He will gradually learn that he must pay attention or be jerked to your side. You can vary the routine by changing speeds, doing turns, figure-eights, and by zig-zagging across the training area.

"HEEL" MEANS "SIT," TOO

To the dog, the command *"Heel"* will also mean that he has to sit in the heel position at your left side when you stop walking — with no additional command from you. As you practice heeling, make him sit whenever you stop, at first using the word *"Sit,"* then with no command at all. He'll soon get the idea and sit down when you stop and wait for the command *"Heel"* to start walking again.

TRAINING TO SIT

Training your dog to sit should be fairly easy. Stand him on your left side, holding the lead fairly short, and command him to *"Sit."* As you give the verbal command, pull up slightly with the lead and push his hindquarters down. Do not let him lie down or stand up. Keep him in a sitting position for a moment, then release the pressure on the lead and praise him. Constantly repeat the command as you hold him in a sitting position, thus fitting the word to the action in his mind. After a while he will begin to get the idea and will sit without your having to push his hindquarters down. When he reaches that stage, insist that he sit on command. If he is slow to obey, slap his hindquarters with your hand to get him down fast. *DO NOT HIT HIM HARD!* Teach him to sit on command facing you as well as when he is at your side. When he begins sitting on command with the lead on, try it with the lead off.

THE "LIE DOWN"

The object of this is to get the dog to lie down either on the verbal command *"Down"* or when you give him the hand signal, your hand raised in front of you, palm down. This is one of the most important parts of training. A well-trained dog will drop on command and stay down whatever the temptation: cat-chasing, car-chasing, or another dog across the street.

Don't start training to lie down until the dog is almost letter-perfect in sitting on command. Then place the dog in a sit, and kneel before him. With both hands, reach forward to his legs and take one front leg in each hand, thumbs up, and holding just below his elbows. Lift his legs slightly off the ground and pull them somewhat out in front of him. Simultaneously, give the command *"Down"* and lower his front legs to the ground.

Hold the dog down and stroke him to let him know that staying down is what you want him to do. This method is far better than forcing a young dog down. Using force can cause him to become very frightened and he will begin to dislike any training. Always talk to your dog and let him know that you are very pleased with him, and soon you will find that you have a happy working dog.

After he begins to get the idea, slide the lead under your left foot and give the command *"Down."* At the same time, pull the lead. This will help get the dog down. Meanwhile, raise your hand in the down signal. Don't expect to accomplish all this in one session. Be patient and work with the dog. He'll cooperate if you show him just what you expect him to do.

THE "STAY"

The next step is to train your dog to stay either in a *"Sit"* or *"Down"* position. Sit him at your side. Give the command *"Stay,"* but be careful not to use his name with this command, because hearing his name may lead him to think that some action is expected of him. If he begins to move, repeat *"Stay"* firmly and hold him down in the sit. Constantly repeat the word *"Stay"* to fix the meaning of that command in his mind. After he has learned to stay for a short time, gradually increase the length of his stay. The hand signal for the stay is a downward sweep of your hand toward the dog's nose, with the palm facing him. While he is sitting, walk around him and stand in front of him. Hold the lead at first; later, drop the lead on the ground in front of him and keep him sitting. If he bolts, scold him and place him back in the same position, repeating the command and all the exercise.

Use some word such as *"Okay"* or *"Up"* to let him know when he can get up, and praise him well for a good performance. As this practice continues, walk farther and farther away from him. Later, try sitting him, giving the command to stay, and then walk out of sight, first for a few seconds, then for longer periods. A well-trained dog should stay where you put him without moving until you come and release him.

Similarly, practice having him stay in the down position, first with you near him, later when you step out of sight.

THE "COME" ON COMMAND

You can train your dog to come when you call him, if you begin when he is young. At first, work with him on lead. Sit the dog, then back away the length of the lead and call him, putting into your voice as much coaxing affection as possible. Give an easy tug on the lead to get him started. When he does come, make a big fuss over him; it might help at this point to give him a small piece of dog candy or food as a reward. He should get the idea soon. You can also move away from him the full length of the lead and call to him something like *"Rex, come,"* then run backward a few steps and stop, making him sit directly in front of you.

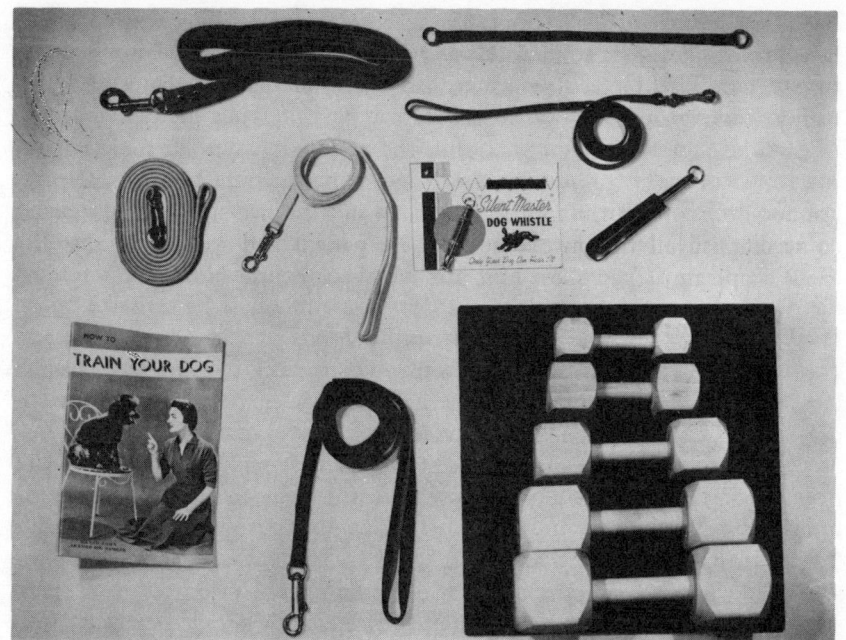

Visit your petshop for all of the training equipment you will need to make your pet a better canine citizen.

Don't be too eager to practice coming on command off lead. Wait until you are certain that you have the dog under perfect control before you try calling him when he's free. Once he gets the idea that he can disobey a command and get away with it, your training program will suffer a serious setback. Keep in mind that your dog's life may depend on his immediate response to a command to come when he is called. If he disobeys off lead, put the lead back on and correct him severely with jerks of the lead.

TEACHING TO COME TO HEEL

The object of this is for you to stand still, say *"Heel,"* and have your dog come right over to you and sit by your left knee in the heel position. If your dog has been trained to sit without command every time you stop, he's ready for this step.

Sit him in front of and facing you and step back one step. Moving only your left foot, pull the dog behind you, then step forward and pull him around until he is in a heel position. You can also have the dog go around by passing the lead behind your back. Use your left heel to straighten him out if he begins to sit behind you or crookedly. This may take a little work, but he will get the idea if you show him just what you want.

THE "STAND"

Your dog should be trained to stand in one spot without moving his feet, and he should allow a stranger to run his hand over his body and legs without showing any resentment or fear. Employ the same method you used in training him to stay on the sit and down. While walking, place your left hand out, palm toward his nose, and command him to stay. His first impulse will be to sit, so be prepared to stop him by placing your hand under his body, near his hindquarters, and holding him until he gets the idea that this is different from the command to sit. Praise him for standing, then walk to the end of the lead. Correct him strongly if he starts to move. Have a stranger approach him and run his hands over the dog's back and down his legs. Keep him standing until you come back to him. Walk around him from his left side, come to the heel position, and make sure that he does not sit until you command him to.

This is a very valuable exercise. If you plan to show your dog he will have learned to stand in a show pose and will allow the judge to examine him.

TRAINING SCHOOLS AND CLASSES

There are dog-training classes in all parts of the country, some sponsored by the local humane society.

If you feel that you lack the time or the skill to train your dog yourself, there are professional dog trainers who will do it for you, but basically dog training is a matter of training YOU and your dog to work together as a team, and if you don't do it yourself you will miss a lot of fun. Don't give up after trying unsuccessfully for a short time. Try a little harder and you and your dog will be able to work things out.

ADVANCED TRAINING AND OBEDIENCE TRIALS

Once you begin training your dog and you see how well he does, you'll probably be bitten by the "obedience bug" — the desire to enter him in obedience trials held under American Kennel Club auspices.

The A.K.C. obedience trials are divided into three classes: Novice, Open, and Utility.

In the Novice Class, the dog will be judged on the following basis:

TEST	MAXIMUM SCORE
Heel on lead	35
Stand for examination	30
Heel free — off lead	45
Recall (come on command)	30
One-minute sit (handler in ring)	30
Three-minute down (handler in ring)	30
Maximum total score	200

If the dog "qualifies" in three shows by earning at least 50% of the points for each test, with a total of at least 170 for the trial, he has earned the Companion Dog degree and the letters C.D. (Companion Dog) are entered after his name in the A.K.C. records.

After the dog has qualified as a C.D., he is eligible to enter the Open Class competition, where he will be judged on this basis:

TEST	MAXIMUM SCORE
Heel free	40
Drop on Recall	30
Retrieve (wooden dumbbell) on flat	25
Retrieve over obstacle (hurdle)	35
Broad jump	20
Three-minute sit (handler out of ring)	25
Five-minute down (handler out of ring)	25
Maximum total score	200

Again he must qualify in three shows for the C.D.X. (Companion Dog Excellent) title and then is eligible for the Utility Class, where he can earn the Utility Dog (U.D.) degree in these rugged tests:

TEST	MAXIMUM SCORE
Scent discrimination (picking up article handled by master from group) Article 1	20
Scent discrimination Article 2	20
Scent discrimination Article 3	20
Seek back (picking up an article dropped by handler)	30
Signal exercise (heeling, etc., on hand signal)	35
Directed jumping (over hurdle and bar jump)	40
Group examination	35
Maximum total score	200

For more complete information about these obedience trials, write for the American Kennel Club's *Regulations and Standards for Obedience Trials*. Dogs that are disqualified from breed shows because of alteration or physical defects are eligible to compete in these trials. Besides the formal A.K.C. obedience trials, there are informal "match" shows in which dogs compete for ribbons and inexpensive trophies. These shows are run by many local fanciers' dog clubs and by all-breed obedience clubs. In many localities the humane society and other groups conduct their own obedience shows. Your local petshop or kennel can keep you informed about such shows in your vicinity, and you will find them listed in the different dog magazines or in the pet column of your local newspaper.

6. Breeding

THE QUESTION OF SPAYING

If you feel that you will never want to raise a litter of purebred puppies, and if you do not wish to risk the possibility of an undesirable mating and surplus mongrel puppies inevitably destined for execution at the local pound, you may want to have your female spayed. Spaying is generally best performed after the female has passed her first heat and before her first birthday: this allows the female to attain the normal female characteristics, while still being young enough to avoid the possible complications encountered when an older female is spayed. A spayed female will remain a healthy, lively pet. You often hear that an altered female will become very fat. However, if you cut down on her food intake, she will not gain weight.

On the other hand, if you wish to show your dog (altered females are disqualified) or enjoy the excitement and feeling of accomplishment of breeding and raising a litter of puppies, particularly in your breed and from your pet, then definitely do not spay.

Male dogs, unlike tomcats, are almost never altered (castrated).

SEXUAL PHYSIOLOGY

Females usually reach sexual maturity (indicated by the first heat cycle, or season) at eight or nine months of age, but sexual maturity may occur as early as six months or as late as thirteen months of age. The average heat cycle (estrus period) lasts for twenty or twenty-one days, and occurs approximately every six months. For about five days immediately preceding the heat period, the female generally displays restlessness and an increased appetite. The vulva, or external genitals, begin to swell. The discharge, which is bright red at the onset and gradually becomes pale pink to straw in color, increases in quantity for several days and then slowly subsides, finally ceasing altogether. The vaginal discharge is subject to much variation: in some bitches it is quite heavy, in others it may never appear, and in some it may be so slight as to go unnoticed.

About eight or nine days after the first appearance of the discharge, the female becomes very playful with other dogs, but will not allow a mating to take place. Anywhere from the tenth or eleventh day, when the discharge has virtually ended and the vulva has softened, to the seventeenth or eighteenth day, the female will accept males and be able to conceive. Many biologists apply the term "heat" only to this receptive phase rather than to the whole estrus, as is commonly done by dog fanciers.

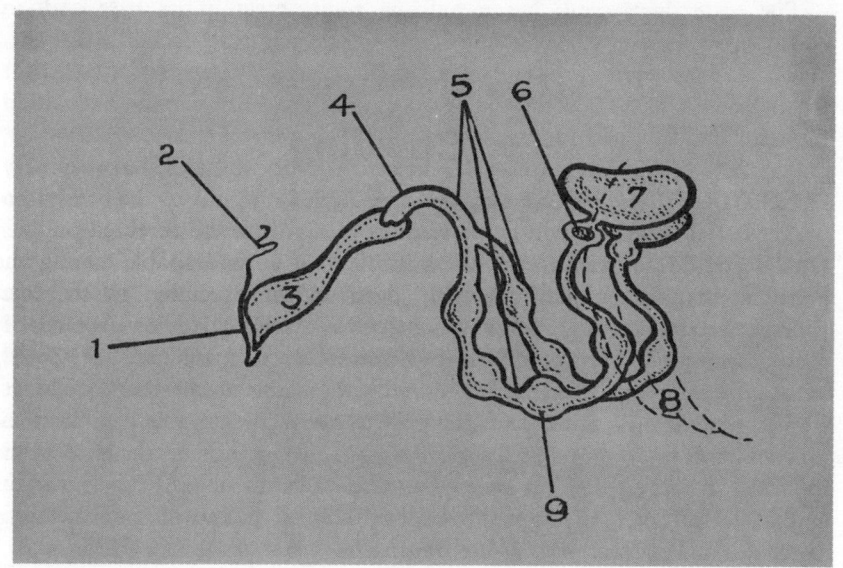

The reproduction system of the bitch: 1, vulva; 2, anus; 3, vagina; 4, cervix; 5, uterus; 6, ovary; 7, kidneys; 8, ribs; 9, fetal lump.

The ova (egg cells) from the female's ovaries are discharged into the oviduct toward the close of the acceptance phase, usually from the sixteenth to eighteenth day. From the eighteenth day until the end of the cycle, the female is still attractive to males, but she will repulse their advances. The entire estrus, however, may be quite variable: in some females vaginal bleeding ends and mating begins on the fourth day; in others, the discharge may continue throughout the entire cycle and the female will not accept males until the seventeenth day or even later.

The male dog — simply referred to by fanciers as the "dog," in contrast to the female, which is referred to as the "bitch" — upon reaching sexual maturity, usually at about six to eight months, is able, like other domesticated mammals, to breed at any time throughout the year.

The testes, the sperm-producing organs of the male, descend from the body cavity into the scrotum at birth. The condition of *cryptorchidism* refers to the retention of one or both testes within the body cavity. A testicle retained within the body cavity is in an environment too hot for it to function normally. A retained testicle may also become cancerous. If only one testicle descends, the dog is known as a *monorchid;* if neither descends, the dog is known as an *anorchid* (dog fanciers, however, refer to a dog with the latter condition as a cryptorchid). A monorchid dog is a fertile animal; an anorchid is sterile.

The male dog's penis has a bulbous enlargement at its base and, in addition, like the penis of a number of other mammals, contains a bone. When mating occurs, pressure on the penis causes a reflex action that fills the bulb with blood, swelling it to about five times its normal size within the female. This locks, or ties, the two animals together. After ejaculation, the animals usually remain tied for fifteen to thirty minutes, but they may separate very quickly or remain together an hour or more, depending on the length of time it takes for the blood to drain from the bulb.

CARE OF THE FEMALE IN ESTRUS

If you have a dog-proof run within your yard, it will be safe to leave your female in season there; if you don't have such a run, she should be shut indoors. Don't leave her alone outside even for a minute; she should be exercised only on lead. If you want to prevent the neighborhood dogs from congregating around your doorstep, as they inevitably will as soon as they discover that your female is in season, take her some distance from the house before you let her relieve herself. Take her in your car to a park or field for a chance to "stretch" her legs (always on lead of course). Keep watch for male dogs, and if one approaches take the female back to the car. After the three weeks are up you can let her out as before with no worry that she can have puppies until her next season.

Some owners find it simpler to board their female at a kennel until her season is over. However, it really is not difficult to watch your female at home. There are various products on the market which are useful at this time. Although the female in season keeps herself quite clean, sometimes she unavoidably stains furniture or rugs. You can buy sanitary belts made especially for dogs at your petshop. Consult your veterinarian for information on pills to be taken to check odor during this period. There also is a pill that prevents the female from coming in season for extended periods, and there are many different types of liquids, powders, and sprays of varying efficiency used to keep male dogs away. However, the one safe rule (whatever products you use) is: keep your bitch away from dogs that could mount her.

SHOULD YOU BREED YOUR MALE?

As with every question, whether or not to use a male dog as a stud has two sides. The arguments for and against using a dog as a stud are often very close to the ridiculous. A classic example would be the tale that once you use a dog as a stud he will lose his value as a show dog or any one of the other functions a dog may have. A sound rule may well be: *if you have a stud who has proven his worth at the shows, place his services out for hire, if only for the betterment of the breed; if your dog is not of show quality, do not use him as a stud.*

Top champion studs can bring their owners many dollars in breeding revenue. If the stud is as good as you feel he is, his services will soon be in great demand. Using a dog as a stud will not lower his value in other functions in any way. Many breeders will permit a male dog to breed an experienced female once, when about a year old, and then they begin to show their stud until he has gained his conformation championship. He is then placed out for hire through advertising in the various bulletins, journals, and show catalogs, and through the stud registers maintained by many pet-shops.

SHOULD YOU BREED YOUR FEMALE?

If you are an amateur and decide to breed your female it would be wise to talk with a breeder and find out all that breeding and caring for puppies entails. You must be prepared to assume the responsibility of caring for the mother through her pregnancy and for the puppies until they are of saleable age. Raising a litter of puppies can be a rewarding experience, but it means work as well as fun, and there is no guarantee of financial profit. As the puppies grow older and require more room and care, the amateur breeder, in desperation, often sells the puppies for much less than they are worth; sometimes he has to give them away. If the cost of keeping the puppies will drain your finances, think twice.

If you have given careful consideration to all these things and still want to breed your female, remember that there is some preparation necessary before taking this step.

WHEN TO BREED

It is usually best to breed in the second or third season. Consider when the puppies will be born and whether their birth and later care will interfere with your work or vacation plans. Gestation period is approximately fifty-eight to sixty-three days. Allow enough time to select the right stud for her. Don't be in a position of having to settle for any available male if she comes into season sooner than expected. Your female will probably be ready to breed twelve days after the first colored discharge. You can usually make arrangements to board her with the owner of the male for a few days to insure her being there at the proper time, or you can take her to be mated and bring her home the same day. If she still appears receptive she may be bred again a day or two later. Some females never show signs of willingness, so it helps to have the experience of a breeder. The second day after the discharge changes color is the proper time; she may be bred for about three days following. For an additional week or so she may have some discharge and attract other dogs by her odor, but she can seldom be bred at this time.

HOW TO SELECT A STUD

Choose a mate for your female with an eye to countering her deficiencies. If possible, both male and female should have **several ancestors in common** within the last two or three generations, as such combinations generally "click" best. The male should have a good show record himself or be the sire of champions. The owner of the stud usually charges a fee for the use of the dog. The fee varies. Payment of a fee does not guarantee a litter, but it does generally confer the right to breed your female again to the stud if she does not have puppies the first time. In some cases the owner of the stud will agree to take a choice puppy in place of a stud fee. You and the owner of the stud should settle all details beforehand, including such questions as what age the puppies should reach before the stud's owner can make his choice, what disposition is made of a single surviving puppy under an agreement by which the stud owner has pick of the litter, and so on. In all cases it is best that the agreement entered into by bitch owner and stud owner be in the form of a written contract.

It is customary for the female to be sent to the male; if the stud dog of your choice lives any distance you will have to make arrangements to have your female shipped to him. The quickest way is by air, and if you call your nearest airport the airline people will give you information as to the best and fastest flight. Some airlines furnish their own crates for shipping, whereas others require that you furnish your own. The owner of the stud will make the arrangements for shipping the female back to you. You have to pay all shipping charges.

PREPARATION FOR BREEDING

Before you breed your female, make sure she is in good health. She should be neither too thin nor too fat. Skin diseases must be cured before breeding; a bitch with skin diseases can pass them on to her puppies. If she has worms she should be wormed before being bred, or within three weeks afterward. It is a good idea to have your veterinarian give her a booster shot for distemper and hepatitis before the puppies are born. This will increase the immunity the puppies receive during their early, most vulnerable period. Choose a dependable veterinarian and rely on him if there is an emergency when your female whelps.

HOW OFTEN SHOULD YOU BREED YOUR FEMALE?

Do not breed your bitch after she reaches six years of age. If you wish to breed her several times while she is young, it is wise to breed her only once a year. In other words, breed her, skip a season, and then breed her again. This will allow her to gain back her full strength between whelpings.

THE IMPORTANCE AND APPLICATION OF GENETICS

Any person attempting to breed dogs should have a basic understanding of the transmission of traits, or characteristics, from the parents to the offspring and some familiarity with the more widely used genetic terms that he will probably encounter. A knowledge of the fundamental mechanics of genetics enables a breeder to better comprehend the passing, complementing, and covering of both good points and faults from generation to generation. It enables him to make a more judicial and scientific decision in selecting potential mates.

Inheritance, fundamentally, is due to the existence of microscopic units, known as *GENES,* present in the cells of all individuals. Genes somehow control the biochemical reactions that occur within the embryo or adult organism. This control results in changing or guiding the development of the organism's characteristics. A "string" of attached genes is known as a *CHROMOSOME.* With a few important exceptions, every chromosome has a partner chromosome carrying a duplicate or equivalent set of genes. Each gene, therefore, has a partner gene, known as an *ALLELE.* The number of different pairs of chromosomes present in the cells of the organism varies with the type of organism: a certain parasitic worm has only one pair, a certain fruit fly has four different pairs, man has 23 different pairs, and your dog has 39 different pairs per cell. Because each chromosome may have many hundreds of genes, a single cell of the body may contain a total of several thousand genes. Heredity is obviously a very complex matter.

In the simplest form of genetic inheritance, one particular gene and its duplicate, or allele, on the partner chromosome control a single characteristic. The presence of freckles in the human skin, for example, is believed to be due to the influence of a single pair of genes.

Each cell of the body contains the specific number of paired chromosomes characteristic of the organism. Because each type of gene is present on both chromosomes of a chromosome pair, *each type of gene is therefore present in duplicate.* The fusion of a sperm cell from the male with an egg cell from the female, as occurs in fertilization, should therefore result in offspring having a *quadruplicate number* (4) of each type of gene. Mating of these individuals would then produce progeny having an *octuplicate number* (8) of each type of gene, and so on. This, however, is normally prevented by a special process. When ordinary body cells prepare to divide to form more tissue, each pair of chromosomes duplicates itself so that there are four partner chromosomes of each kind instead of only two. When the cell divides, two of the four partners, or one pair, go into each new cell. This process, known as *MITOSIS,* insures that each new body cell contains the proper number of chromosomes. Reproductive cells (sperm cell and egg cells), however, undergo a special kind of division known as *MEIOSIS.* In meiosis, the chromosome pairs do *not* duplicate themselves, and thus when the reproductive cells reach the final dividing stage only one chromosome, or one-half of the pair, goes into each new reproductive cell. Each reproductive cell, therefore, has only half the normal number of chromosomes. These are referred to as *HAPLOID* cells, in contrast to *DIPLOID* cells, which have the full number of chromosomes.

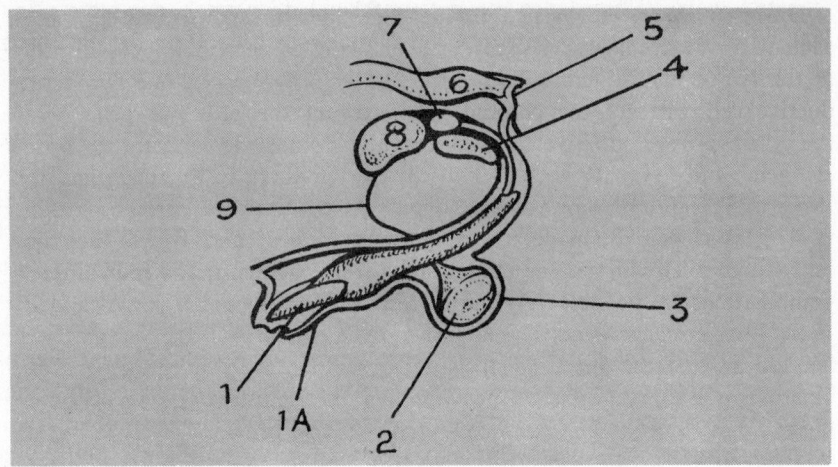

The reproductive system of a male: 1a, sheath; 1, penis; 2, testicle; 3, scrotum; 4, pelvic bone; 5, anus; 6, rectum; 7, prostate; 8, bladder; 9, vas deferens.

When the haploid sperm cell fuses with the haploid egg cell in fertilization, the resulting offspring has the normal diploid number of chromosomes.

If both partner genes, or alleles, affect the trait in an identical manner, the genes are said to be *HOMOZYGOUS*, but if one affects the character in a manner different from the other gene, or allele, the genes are said to be *HETEROZYGOUS*. For example, in the pair of genes affecting eye color in humans, if each gene of the pair produces blue eyes, the genes (and also the person carrying the genes) are said to be homozygous for blue eyes. If, however, one gene of the pair produces blue eyes, while the other gene, or allele, produces brown eyes, they are said to be heterozygous. The presence of heterozygous genes raises the question, *"Will the offspring have blue eyes or brown eyes?"* which in turn introduces another genetic principle: *DOMINANCE* and *RECESSIVENESS*.

If one gene of a pair can block the action of its partner, or allele, while still producing its own affect, that gene is said to be *dominant* over its allele. Its allele, on the other hand, is said to be recessive. In the case of heterozygous genes for eye color, the brown eye gene is dominant over the recessive blue eye gene, and the offspring therefore will have brown eyes. Much less common is the occurrence of gene pairs in which neither gene is completely dominant over the other. This, known as *INCOMPLETE* or *PARTIAL DOMINANCE*, results in a blending of the opposing influences. In cattle, if a homozygous (pure) red bull is mated with a homozygous (pure) white cow, the calf will be roan, a blending of red and white hairs in its coat, rather than either all red or all white.

During meiosis, or division of the reproductive (sperm and egg) cells, each pair of chromosomes splits, and one-half of each pair goes into one of the two new cells. Thus, in the case of eye color genes, one new reproductive cell will get the chromosome carrying the blue eye gene, while the other new reproductive cell will get the chromosome carrying the brown eye gene, and so on for each pair of chromosomes. If an organism has only two pairs of chromosomes — called pair A, made up of chromosomes A_1 and A_2, and pair B, made up of chromosomes B_1 and B_2 — each new reproductive cell will get one chromosome from each pair, and four different combinations are possible: A_1 and B_1; A_1 and B_2; A_2 and B_1, or A_2 and B_2. If the blue eye gene is on A_1, the brown eye gene on A_2, the gene for curly hair on B_1 and the gene for straight hair on B_2, each of the above combinations will exert a different genetic effect on the offspring. This different grouping of chromosomes in the new reproductive cell as a result of meiotic cell division is known as *INDEPENDENT ASSORTMENT* and is one reason why variation occurs in the offspring. In the dog, with 39 pairs of chromosomes, the possibilities of variation through independent assortment are tremendous.

But variation does not end here. For example, if two dominant genes, such as the genes for brown eyes and dark hair, were on the same chromosome, all brown-eyed people would have dark hair. Yet in instances where such joined or *LINKED* genes do occur, the two characteristics do not always appear together in the same offspring. This is due to a process known as *CROSS-OVER* or *RECOMBINATION*. Recombination is the mutual exchange of corresponding blocks of genes between the two chromosomes in a pair. That is, during cell division, the two chromosomes may exchange their tip sections or other corresponding segments. If the segments exchanged contain the eye color genes, the brown eye gene will be transferred from the chromosome carrying the dark hair gene to the chromosome carrying the light hair gene, and then brown eyes will occur with light hair, provided that the individual is homozygous for the recessive light hair gene.

Another important source of variation is *MUTATION*. In mutation, a gene becomes altered, such as by exposure to irradiation, and exerts a different effect than it did before. Most mutations are harmful to the organism, and some may result in death. Offspring carrying mutated genes and showing the effects of these mutations are known as *MUTANTS* or *SPORTS*. Mutation also means that instead of only two alleles for eye color, such as brown and blue, there may now be three or more (gray, black, etc.) creating a much larger source for possible variation in the offspring.

Further complications in the transmission and appearance of genetic traits are the phenomena known as *EPISTASIS* and *PLEIOTROPY*. Epistasis refers to a gene exerting influence on genes other than its own allele.

In all-white red-eyed (albino) guinea pigs, for example, the gene controlling intensity of color is epistatic to any other color gene and prevents that gene from producing its effect. Thus, even if a gene for red spots were present in the cells of the guinea pig, the color intensity gene would prevent the red spots from appearing in the guinea pig's white coat. *Pleiotropy* refers to the fact that a single gene may control a number of characteristics. In the fruit fly, for example, the gene that controls eye color may also affect the structure of certain body parts and even the lifespan of the insect.

One special pair of chromosomes is known as the sex chromosomes. In man, dog, and other mammals, these chromosomes are of two types, designated as X and Y. Under normal conditions, a mammal carrying two X-type sex chromosomes is a female, whereas a mammal carrying one X-type and one Y-type is a male. Females, therefore, have only X chromosomes and can only contribute X chromosomes to the offspring, but the male may contribute either an X or a Y.

If the male's sperm carrying an X chromosome fertilizes the female's egg cell (X), the offspring (XX) will be female; if a sperm carrying a Y chromosome fertilizes the egg (X), the offspring (XY) will be male. It is the male, therefore, that determines the sex of the offspring in mammals.

Traits controlled by genes present on the sex chromosome, and which appear in only one sex, are said to be *SEX LINKED*. If, for example, a rare recessive gene occurs on the X chromosome, it cannot exert its effect in the female because the dominant allele on the other X chromosome will counteract it. In the male, however, there is no second X chromosome, and if the Y chromosome cannot offer any countereffect, the recessive character will appear. There are also *SEX-LIMITED* characteristics: these appear primarily or solely in one sex, but the genes for these traits are not carried on the sex chromosomes. Sex-limited traits appear when genes on other chromosomes exert their effect in the proper hormonal (male or female) environment. Sex-linked and sex-limited transmission is how a trait may skip a generation, by being passed from grandfather to grandson through a mother in which the trait, though present, does not show.

In dealing with the simplest form of heredity — one gene effecting one character — there is an expected ratio of the offspring displaying the character to those who do not display it, depending upon the genetic makeup of the parents. If a parent is homozygous for a character, such as blue eyes, it makes no difference which half of the chromosome pair enters the new reproductive cell, because each chromosome carries the gene for blue eyes. If a parent is heterozygous, however, one reproductive cell will receive the brown eye gene while the other will receive the blue eye gene. If both parents are homozygous for blue eyes, all the offspring will receive two blue eye genes, and all will have blue eyes. If a parent is homozygous for blue eyes, and the other parent is homozygous for brown eyes, all the offspring will be heterozygous, receiving one brown eye gene and one blue eye gene, and because brown is dominant, all will have brown eyes. If both parents are heterozygous, both the blue eye gene and the brown eye gene from one parent have an equal likelihood of ending up with either the blue eye or the brown eye gene from the other parent. This results in a ratio of two heterozygous offspring to the one homozygous for brown eyes and one homozygous for blue eyes, giving a total genetic, or genotypic, ratio of $2:1:1$ or, as it is more commonly arranged, $1:2:1$. As the two heterozygous as well as the homozygous brown eye offspring will have brown eyes, the ratio of brown eyes to blue eyes (or phenotypic ratio) will be $3:1$.

If one parent is heterozygous and the other parent is homozygous for the recessive gene for blue eyes, half of the offspring will be homozygous for blue eyes and will have blue eyes, but the other half of the offspring will be heterozygous and have brown eyes. (Here both the genotypic and phenotypic ratio is $1:1$.)

If the homozygous parent, however, has the dominant gene (brown eyes), half of the offspring will be heterozygous and half will be homozygous, as before, but all will have brown eyes. By repeated determinations of these ratios in the offspring, geneticists are able to analyze the genetic makeup of the parents.

Before leaving heredity, it might be well to explain the difference between inbreeding, outcrossing, line breeding, and similar terms. Basically, there are only inbreeding and outbreeding. Inbreeding, however, according to its intensity, is usually divided into inbreeding proper and line breeding. Inbreeding proper is considered to be the mating of very closely related individuals, generally within the immediate family, but this is sometimes extended to include matings to first cousins and grandparents. Line breeding is the mating of more distantly related animals, that is, animals, not immediately related to each other but having a common ancestor, such as the same grandsire or great-grandsire. Outbreeding is divided into outcrossing, which is the mating of dogs from different families within the same breed, and cross-breeding, which is mating purebred dogs from different breeds.

From the foregoing discussion of genetics, it should be realized that the theory of telegony, which states that the sire of one litter can influence future litters sired by other studs, is simply not true; it is possible, however, if several males mate with a female during a single estrus cycle, that the various puppies in the litter may have different sires (but not two sires for any one puppy). It should also be realized that blood does not really enter into the transmission of inheritance, although people commonly speak of "bloodlines," "pure-blooded," etc.

7. Care of the Mother and Family

PRENATAL CARE OF THE FEMALE

You can expect the puppies nine weeks from the day of breeding, although 58 days is as common as 63. During this time the female should receive normal care and exercise. If she is overweight, don't increase her food at first; excess weight at whelping time is not good. If she is on the thin side, build her up, giving her a morning meal of cereal and egg yolk. Consult your veterinarian as to increasing her vitamins and mineral supplement. During the last weeks the puppies grow enormously, and the mother will have little room for food and less appetite. Divide her meals into smaller portions and feed her more ofen. If she loses her appetite, tempt her with meat, liver, chicken, etc.

As she grows heavier, eliminate violent exercise and jumping. Do not eliminate exercise entirely, as walking is beneficial to the female in whelp, and mild exercise will maintain her muscle tone in preparation for the birth. Weigh your female after breeding and keep a record of her weight each week thereafter. Groom your bitch daily — some females have a slight discharge during gestation, more prevalent during the last two weeks, so wash the vulva with warm water daily. Usually, by the end of the fifth week you can notice a broadening across her loins, and her breasts become firmer. By the end of the sixth week your veterinarian can tell you whether or not she is pregnant.

PREPARATION OF WHELPING QUARTERS

Prepare a whelping box at least a week before the puppies are to arrive and allow the mother-to-be to sleep there overnight or to spend some time in it during the day to become accustomed to it. She is then less likely to try to have her litter under the front porch or in the middle of your bed.

The box should have a wooden floor. Sides should be high enough to keep the puppies in but low enough to allow the mother to get out after she has fed them. Layers of newspapers spread over the whole area will make excellent bedding and will be absorbent enough to keep the surface warm and dry. They should be removed when wet or soiled and replaced with another thick layer. An old quilt or blanket is more comfortable for the mother and makes better footing for the nursing puppies, at least during the first week, than slippery newspaper. The quilt should be secured firmly.

SUPPLIES TO HAVE ON HAND

As soon as you have the whelping box prepared, set up the nursery by collecting the various supplies you will need when the puppies arrive. You should have the following items on hand: a box lined with towels for the puppies, a heating pad or hot water bottle to keep the puppy box warm, a pile of clean terrycloth towels or washcloths to remove membranes and to dry puppies, a stack of folded newspapers, a roll of paper towels, vaseline, rubber gloves, soap, iodine, muzzle, cotton balls, a small pair of blunt scissors to cut umbilical cords (stick them into an open bottle of alcohol so they keep freshly sterilized), a rectal thermometer, white thread, a flashlight in case the electricity goes off, a waste container, and a scale for weighing each puppy at birth.

It is necessary that the whelping room be warm and free from drafts, because puppies are delivered wet from the mother. Keep a little notebook and pencil handy so you can record the duration of the first labor and the time between the arrival of each puppy. If there is trouble in whelping, this is the information that the veterinarian will want. Keep his telephone number handy in case you have to call him in an emergency, and warn him to be prepared for an emergency, should you need him.

WHELPING

Be prepared for the actual whelping several days in advance. Usually the female will tear up papers, try to dig nests, refuse food, and generally act restless and nervous. These may be false alarms; the real test is her temperature, which will drop to below 100° about twelve hours before whelping. Take her temperature rectally at a set time each day, starting about a week before she is due to whelp. After her temperature goes down, keep her constantly with you or put her in the whelping box and stay in the room with her. She will seem anxious and look to you for reassurance. Be prepared to remove the membranes covering the puppy's head if the mother fails to do this, for the puppy could smother otherwise.

The mother should start licking the puppy as soon as it is out of the sac, thus drying and stimulating it, but if she does not perform this task you can do it with a soft rough towel, instead. The afterbirth should follow the birth of each puppy, attached to the puppy by the umbilical cord. Watch to make sure that each is expelled, for retaining this material can cause infection. The mother probably will eat the afterbirth after biting the cord. One or two will not hurt her; they stimulate milk supply as well as labor for remaining puppies. Too many, however, can make her lose her appetite for the food she needs to feed her puppies and regain her strength, so remove the rest of them along with the soiled newspapers, and keep the box dry and clean to relieve her anxiety.

If a puppy does not start breathing, wrap him in a towel, hold him upside down with his head toward the ground, and shake him vigorously. If he still does not breathe, rub his ribs briskly; if this also fails, administer artificial respiration by compressing the ribs about twenty times per minute.

If the mother does not bite the cord, or bites it too close to the body, you should take over the job to prevent an umbilical hernia. Cut the cord a short distance from the body with your blunt scissors. Put a drop of iodine on the end of the cord; it will dry up and fall off in a few days.

The puppies should follow each other at regular intervals, but deliveries can be as short as five minutes or as long as two hours apart. A puppy may be presented backwards; if the mother does not seem to be in trouble, do not interfere. But if enough of the puppy is outside the birth canal, use a rough towel and help her by pulling gently on the puppy. Pull only when she pushes. A rear-first, or breech, birth can cause a puppy to strangle on its own umbilical cord, so don't let the mother struggle too long. Breech birth is quite common.

When you think all the puppies have been whelped, have your veterinarian examine the mother to determine if all the afterbirths have been expelled. He will probably give her an injection to be certain that the uterus is clean, a shot of calcium for prevention of eclampsia, and possibly an injection of penicillin to prevent infection.

RAISING THE PUPPIES

Hold each puppy to a breast as soon as you have dried him. This will be an opportunity to have a good meal without competition. Then place him in the small box that you have prepared so he will be out of his mother's way while she is whelping. Keep a record of birth weights and take weekly readings thereafter so that you will have an accurate account of the puppies' growth. After the puppies have arrived, take the mother outside for a walk and a drink, and then leave her to take care of them. Offer her a dish of vanilla ice cream or milk with corn syrup in it. She usually will eat lying down while the puppies are nursing and will appreciate the coolness of the ice cream during warm weather or in a hot room. She will not want to stay away from her puppies more than a minute or two the first few weeks. Be sure to keep water available at all times, and feed her milk or broth frequently, as she needs liquids to produce milk. To encourage her to eat, offer her the foods she likes best, until she "asks" to be fed without your tempting her. She will soon develop a ravenous appetite and should be fed whenever she is hungry.

Be sure that all the puppies are getting enough to eat. Cut their claws with special dog "nail" clippers, as they grow rapidly and scratch the mother as the puppies nurse. Normally the puppies should be completely weaned by six weeks, although you may start to give them supplementary feedings at three weeks. They will find it easier to lap semi-solid food.

As the puppies grow up, the mother will go into the box only to nurse them, first sitting up and then standing. To dry up her milk supply completely, keep her away from her puppies for longer periods. After a few days of part-time nursing she will be able to stay away for much longer periods of time, and then completely. The little milk left will be resorbed.

When the puppies are five weeks old, consult your veterinarian about temporary shots to protect them against distemper and hepatitis; it is quite possible for dangerous infectious germs to reach them even though you keep their living quarters sanitary. You can expect the puppies to need at least one worming before they are ready to go to their new homes, so take a stool sample to your veterinarian before they are three weeks old. If one puppy has worms, all should be wormed. Follow your veterinarian's advice.

The puppies may be put outside, unless it is too cold, as soon as their eyes are open (about ten days), and they will benefit from the sunlight. A rubber mat or newspapers underneath their box will protect them from cold or dampness.

HOW TO TAKE CARE OF A LARGE LITTER

The size of a litter varies greatly. If your bitch has a large litter she may have trouble feeding all of the puppies. You can help her by preparing an extra puppy box. Leave half the litter with the mother and the other half in a warm place, changing their places at two-hour intervals at first. Later you may change them less frequently, leaving them all together except during the day. Try supplementary feeding, too, as soon as their eyes are open.

CAESAREAN SECTION

If your female goes into hard labor and is not able to give birth within two hours, you will know that there is something wrong. Call your veterinarian for advice. Some females must have Caesarean sections (taking puppies from the mother by surgery), but don't be alarmed if your dog has to undergo this. The operation is relatively safe. She can be taken to the veterinarian, operated on, and then be back in her whelping box at home within three hours, with all puppies nursing normally a short time later.

8. Health

WATCHING YOUR PUPPY'S HEALTH

First, don't be frightened by the number of diseases a dog can contract. The majority of dogs never get any of them. Don't become a dog-hypochondriac. All dogs have days when they feel lazy and want to lie around doing nothing. For the few diseases that you might be concerned about, remember that your veterinarian is your dog's best friend. When you first get your puppy, select a veterinarian who you feel is qualified to treat dogs. He will get to know your dog and will be glad to have you consult him for advice. A dog needs little medical care, but that little is essential to his good health and well-being. He needs:

1. Proper diet at regular hours
2. Clean, roomy housing
3. Daily exercise
4. Companionship and love
5. Frequent grooming
6. Regular check-ups by your veterinarian

THE USEFUL THERMOMETER

Almost every serious ailment shows itself by an increase in the dog's body temperature. If your dog acts lifeless, looks dull-eyed, and gives the impression of illness, check his temperature by using a rectal thermometer. Hold the dog and insert the thermometer, which should be lubricated with vaseline, and take a reading. The average normal temperature is 101.5° F. Excitement may raise this value slightly, but any rise of more than a few points is a cause for alarm. Consult your veterinarian.

FIRST AID

In general, a dog will heal his wounds by licking them. If he swallows anything harmful, chances are that he will throw it up. But it will probably make you feel better to help him if he is hurt, so treat his wounds as you would your own. Wash out the dirt and apply an antiseptic. If you are afraid that your dog has swallowed poison and you can't get to the veterinarian fast enough, try to induce vomiting by giving him a strong solution of salt water or mustard and water. Amateur diagnosis is dangerous, because the symptoms of so many dog diseases are alike. Too many people wait too long to take their dog to the doctor.

IMPORTANCE OF INOCULATIONS

With the proper series of inoculations, your dog will be almost completely protected against disease. However, it occasionally happens that the shot does not take, and sometimes a different form of the virus appears against which your dog may not be protected.

DISTEMPER

Probably the most virulent of all dog diseases is distemper. Young dogs are most susceptible to it, although it may affect dogs of all ages. The dog will lose his appetite, seem depressed, chilled, and run a fever. Often he will have a watery discharge from his eyes and nose. Unless treated promptly, the disease goes into advanced stages with infections of the lungs, intestines, and nervous system, and dogs that recover may be left with some impairment such as paralysis, convulsions, a twitch, or some other defect, usually spastic in nature. The best protection against this is very early inoculation with a series of permanent shots and a booster shot each year thereafter.

HEPATITIS

Veterinarians report an increase in the spread of this viral disease in recent years, usually with younger dogs as the victims. The initial symptoms — drowsiness, vomiting, great thirst, loss of appetite, and a high temperature — closely resemble those of distemper. These symptoms are often accompanied by swellings of the head, neck, and abdomen. The disease strikes quickly; death may occur in just a few hours. Protection is afforded by injection with a vaccine recently developed.

LEPTOSPIROSIS

This disease is caused by bacteria that live in stagnant or slow-moving water. It is carried by rats and dogs; infection is begun by the dog's licking substances contaminated by the urine or feces of infected animals. The symptoms are diarrhea and a yellowish-brown discoloration of the jaws, tongue, and teeth, caused by an inflammation of the kidneys. This disease can be cured if caught in time, but it is best to ward it off with a vaccine which your veterinarian can administer along with the distemper shots.

RABIES

This is an acute disease of the dog's central nervous system. It is spread by infectious saliva transmitted by the bite of an infected animal. Rabies is generally manifested in one of two classes of symptoms. The first is "furious rabies," in which the dog shows a period of melancholy or depression, then irritation, and finally paralysis. The first period lasts from a few hours to several days. During this time the dog is cross and will change his position often. He loses his appetite for food and begins to lick, bite, and swallow foreign objects. During the irritative phase the dog is spasmodically wild and has impulses to run away. He acts in a fearless manner and runs and bites at everything in sight. If he is caged or confined he will fight at the bars, often breaking teeth or fracturing his jaw. His bark becomes a peculiar howl. In the final, or paralytic, stage, the animal's lower jaw becomes paralyzed and hangs down; he walks with a stagger and saliva drips from his mouth. Within four to eight days after the onset of paralysis, the dog dies.

The second class of symptoms is referred to as "dumb rabies" and is characterized by the dog's walking in a bearlike manner, head down. The lower jaw is paralyzed and the dog is unable to bite. Outwardly it may seem as though he had a bone caught in his throat.

Even if your pet should be bitten by a rabid dog or other animal, he probably can be saved if you get him to the veterinarian in time for a series of injections. However, after the symptoms have appeared no cure is possible. But remember that an annual rabies inoculation is almost certain protection against rabies. If you suspect your dog of rabies, notify your local Health Department. A rabid dog is a danger to all who come near him.

COUGHS, COLDS, BRONCHITIS, PNEUMONIA

Respiratory diseases may affect the dog because he is forced to live under man-made conditions rather than in his natural environment. Being subjected to cold or a draft after a bath, sleeping near an air conditioner or in the path of a fan or near a radiator can cause respiratory ailments. The symptoms are similar to those in humans. The germs of these diseases, however, are different and do not affect both dogs and humans, so they cannot be infected by each other. Treatment is much the same as for a child with the same type of illness. Keep the dog warm, quiet, and well fed. Your veterinarian has antibiotics and other remedies to help the dog recover.

INTERNAL PARASITES

There are four common internal parasites that may infect your dog. These are roundworms, hookworms, whipworms, and tapeworms. The first three can be diagnosed by laboratory examination; the presence of tapeworms is determined by seeing segments in the stool or attached to the hair around the tail. Do not under any circumstances attempt to worm your dog without the advice of your veterinarian. After first determining what type of worm or worms are present, he will advise you of the best method of treatment.

EXTERNAL PARASITES

The dog that is groomed regularly and provided with clean sleeping quarters should not be troubled by fleas, ticks, or lice. If the dog should become infested with any of these parasites, he should be treated with a medicated dip bath or the new oral medications that are presently available.

SKIN AILMENTS

Any persistent scratching may indicate an irritation. Whenever you groom your dog, look for the reddish spots that may indicate eczema, mange, or fungal infection. Rather than treating your dog yourself, take him to the

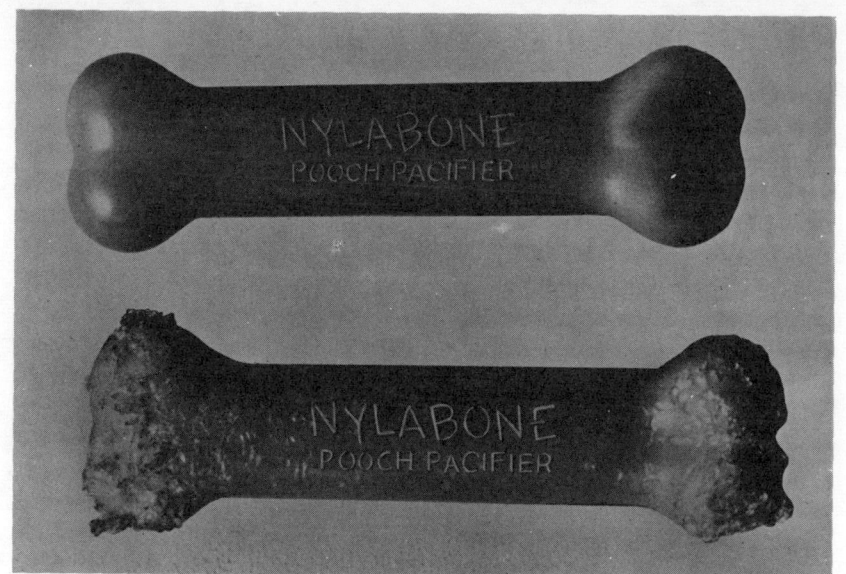

NYLABONE® is a necessity that is available at your local petshop (not in supermarkets). The puppy or grown dog chews the hambone flavored nylon into a frilly dog toothbrush, massaging his gums and cleaning his teeth as he plays. Veterinarians highly recommend this product . . . but beware of cheap imitations which might splinter or break.

veterinarian, as some of the conditions may be difficult to eradicate and can cause permanent damage to his coat.

EYES, EARS, TEETH, AND CLAWS

If you notice foreign matter collecting in the corners of your dog's eyes, wipe it out with a piece of cotton or tissue. If there is a discharge, check with your veterinarian.

Examine your dog's ears daily. Remove all visible wax, using a piece of cotton dipped in a boric acid solution or a solution of equal parts of water and hydrogen peroxide. Be gentle and don't probe into the ear, but just clean the parts you can see.

Don't give your dog bones to chew: they can choke him or puncture his intestines. Today veterinarians and dog experts recommend Nylabone, a synthetic bone manufactured by a secret process, that can't splinter or break even when pounded by a hammer. Nylabone will keep puppies from chewing furniture, aid in relieving the aching gums of a teething pup, and act as a toothbrush for the older dog, preventing the accumulation of tartar. Check your dog's mouth regularly and, as he gets older, have your veterinarian clean his teeth twice a year.

To clip your dog's claws, use specially designed clippers that are available at your petshop. Never take off too much of the claw, as you might

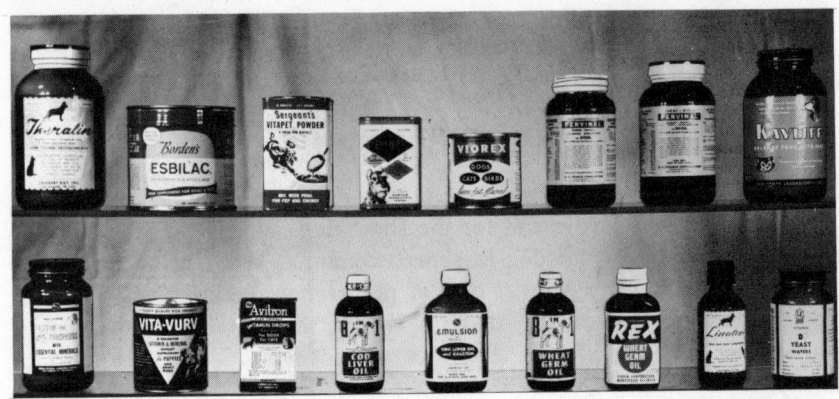

Active dogs and breeding bitches need food supplements. Visit your petshop for fresh vitamins and minerals to be added to your dog's diet.

cut the quick, which is sensitive and will bleed. Be particularly careful when you cut claws in which the quick is not visible. If you have any doubts about being able to cut your dog's claws, have your veterinarian or petshop do it periodically.

CARE OF THE AGED DOG

With the increased knowledge and care available, there is no reason why your dog should not live to a good old age. As the years go by he may need a little additional care. Remember that an excessively fat dog is not healthy, particularly as he grows older, so limit the older dog's food accordingly. He needs exercise as much as ever, although his heart cannot bear the strain of sudden and violent exertion. Failing eyesight or hearing means lessened awareness of dangers, so you must protect him more than ever.

Should you decide at this time to get a puppy, to avoid being without a dog when your old friend is no longer with you, be very careful how you introduce the puppy. He naturally will be playful and will expect the older dog to respond to his advances. Sometimes the old dog will get a new lease on life from a new puppy, but he may be consumed with jealousy. Do not give the newcomer the attention that formerly was exclusively the older dog's. Feed them apart, and show your old friend that you still love him the most; the puppy, not being accustomed to individual attention, will not mind sharing your love.

9. Showing

There is no greater pleasure for the owner than showing a beautiful dog perfectly groomed and trained for the show ring. Whether he wins or not, it is gratifying to show a dog in superb condition, one that is a credit to your training and care. A great deal of preparation, both for you and your dog, is needed before the day that you do any serious winning. Showing is not so easy as it looks, even if you have a magnificent dog. He must be presented to the judge so that all of his good points are shown to advantage. This requires practice in gaiting, daily grooming from puppyhood, and the proper diet to make him sound in body.

When you buy your puppy you probably will think he is the best in the country and possibly in the world, but before you enter the highly competitive world of dog shows, get some unbiased expert opinion. As your dog matures, compare him with the standard of his breed. Visit a few dog shows as a spectator and make mental notes of what is required of the handlers and dogs. Watch how the experienced handlers manage their dogs to bring out their best points.

TYPES OF DOG SHOWS

There are various types of dog shows. The American Kennel Club sanctioned matches are shows at which purebred dogs may compete, but not for championship points. These are excellent for you to enter to accustom you and your dog to showing. If your dog places in a few match shows, then you might seriously consider entering the big-time shows. An American Kennel Club all-breed show is one at which purebred dogs compete for championship points. An American Kennel Club specialty show is for one breed only. It may be held in conjunction with an all-breed show (by designating the classes at that show as its specialty show) or it may be held entirely apart. Obedience trials are different in that in them the dog is judged according to his obedience and ability to perform, not by his conformation to the breed standard.

There are two types of championship conformation shows: *benched* and *unbenched*. At a benched show your dog must be on his appointed bench during the advertised hours of the show's duration. He may be removed from the bench only to be taken to the exercise pen or to be groomed (an hour before showing) in an area designated for handlers to set up their crates and grooming tables. At an unbenched show your car may serve as a bench for your dog.

To become a champion your dog must win fifteen points in competition with other dogs; a portion of the fifteen points must be awarded as major point wins (three to five points) under different judges.

HOW TO ENTER

If your dog is purebred and registered with the AKC — or eligible for registration — you may enter him in the appropriate show class for which his age, sex, and previous show record qualify him. You will find coming shows listed in the different dog magazines or at your petshop. Write to the secretary of the show, asking for the premium list. When you receive the entry form, fill it in carefully and send it back with the required entry fee. Then, before the show, you should receive your exhibitor's pass, which will admit you and your dog to the show. Here are the five official show classes:

PUPPY CLASS: Open to dogs at least six months and not more than twelve months of age. Limited to dogs whelped in the United States and Canada.

NOVICE CLASS: Open to dogs six months of age or older that have never won a first prize in any class other than the puppy class, and less than three first prizes in the novice class itself. Limited to dogs whelped in the United States or Canada.

BRED BY EXHIBITOR CLASS: Open to all dogs, except champions, six months of age or over which are exhibited by the same person, or his immediate family, or kennel that was the recognized breeder on the records of the American Kennel Club.

AMERICAN-BRED CLASS: Open to dogs that are not champions, six months of age or over, whelped in the United States after a mating which took place in the United States.

OPEN CLASS: Open to dogs six months of age or over, with no exceptions.

In addition there are local classes, the Specials Only class, and brace and team entries.

For full information on dog shows, read the book *HOW TO SHOW YOUR OWN DOG,* by Virginia Tuck Nichols. (T.F.H.)

ADVANCED PREPARATION

Before you go to a show your dog should be trained to gait at a trot beside you, with head up and in a straight line. In the ring you will have to gait your dog around the edge with other dogs and then individually up and down the center runner. In addition the dog must stand for examination by the judge, who will look at him closely and feel his head and body structure. He should be taught to stand squarely, hind feet slightly back, head up on the alert. Showing requires practice training sessions in advance. Get a friend to act as judge and set the dog up and "show" him a few minutes every day.

Sometime before the show, give your dog a bath so he will look his best. Get together all the things you will need to take to the show. You will want to take a water dish and a bottle of water for your dog (so he won't be affected by a change in drinking water). Take your show lead, bench chain (if it is a benched show), combs and brush, and the identification ticket sent by the show superintendent, noting the time you must be there and the place where the show will be held, as well as the time of judging.

THE DAY OF THE SHOW

Don't feed your dog the morning of the show, or give him at most a light meal. He will be more comfortable in the car on the way, and will show more enthusiastically. When you arrive at the show grounds, find out where he is to be benched and settle him there. Your bench or stall number is on your identification ticket, and the breed name will be on placards fastened to the ends of the row of benches. Once you have your dog securely fastened to his stall by a bench chain (use a bench crate instead of a chain if you prefer), locate the ring where your dog will be judged (the number and time of showing will be on the program of judging which came with your ticket). After this you may want to take your dog to the exercise ring to relieve himself, and give him a small drink of water. Your dog will have been groomed before the show, but give him a final brushing just before going into the show ring. When your breed judging is called, it is your responsibility to be at the ringside ready to go in. The steward will give you an armband which has on it the number of your dog.

Then, as you step into the ring, try to keep your knees from knocking! Concentrate on your dog and before you realize it you'll be out again, perhaps back with the winners of each class for more judging and finally, with luck, it will be over and you'll have a ribbon and trophy — and, of course, the most wonderful dog in the world.

BIBLIOGRAPHY

PS-606 DOLLARS IN DOGS, by Leon F. Whitney, D.V.M. The 26 chapters of this beautifully useful book tell you—frankly and clearly—how you can make money in the dog field. Every avenue to profit through dogs is explored thoroughly by Dr. Whitney, famous veterinarian and breeder. There are no punches pulled in the discussions of money-making opportunities available to everyone who wants to profit through his connection with canines. A real career-builder, 254 pages of solid and practical information, illustrated.
ISBN #0-87666-290-4
8½ x 5½ 255 pages 60 black & white photos

PS-684 DOG HOROSCOPE—YOUR DOG NEEDS A BIRTHDAY. Probably the most clever and entertaining dog book ever published. Illustrated in color, readers are in for 64 pages of informative amusement, and you don't have to be an astrology fan to enjoy it.
ISBN #0-87666-317-X
8 x 5½ 64 pages 14 line illustrations

PS-607 HOW TO SHOW YOUR OWN DOG, by Virginia Tuck Nichols, paves the highroad to success in the fascinating and steadily growing avocation of exhibiting dogs. All of the intricacies of the show ring are explained in detail, coupled with wonderfully explicit treatments of the basics of dog shows; terms and definitions, how a champion is made, getting ready for the show, AKC rules and regulations, etc. Plus a bonus chapter on the tricks of the trade. In all, 254 well-illustrated pages that make winning in the dog show ring easier and a lot more fun.
ISBN #0-87666-390-0
8½ x 5½ 254 pages 136 black & white photos 10 line illustrations

H-925 DOG BREEDERS' HANDBOOK, by Ernest H. Hart. Here is the most complete and authoritative book on breeding ever written. In layman's language it clarifies all areas of this very necessary but often misunderstood subject. Beautifully presented and authored by a professional writer and recognized dog authority, the written word is augmented by profuse and pertinent illustrations.
ISBN #0-87666-286-6
85 black & white photos 12 line illustrations

PS-644 HOW TO TRAIN YOUR DOG, by Ernest H. Hart. Any dog is a better dog when well-trained. With the help of this book, any owner can do a first class job of training his dog. Fully and completely illustrated, the author takes you step by advancing step through the various areas of training. Many vital new concepts of training are advanced and discussed in this invaluable book. Color and black and white illustrations.
ISBN #0-87666-284-X
8½ x 5½ 107 pages 95 black & white photos 31 color photos

H-934 DOG OWNER'S ENCYCLOPEDIA OF VETERINARY MEDICINE, by Dr. Allan Hart. Here is a book that will become, next to his pet itself, the truest friend a dog-owner has. Page after page and chapter after chapter of valuable, pertinent information that allows an owner to make sure that his pet is given the best of care at all times. Easy to read yet brilliantly informative, this big book is a must.
ISBN #0-87666-287-4
8 x 5½ 186 pages 61 black & white photos 25 line illustrations